Be a
DISCIPLE,
Make a
DISCIPLE

Blessings in
Christ –
Ellie
2 Peter 3:18

Be a
DISCIPLE,
Make a
DISCIPLE

A Bible
STUDY

ELLIE M. LITTLETON

REDEMPTION
PRESS

Published by Redemption Press, PO Box 427, Enumclaw, WA 98022
Toll Free (844) 2REDEEM (273-3336)

Redemption Press is honored to present this title in partnership with the author. The views expressed or implied in this work are those of the author. Redemption Press provides our imprint seal representing design excellence, creative content, and high-quality production.

ISBN 13: 978-1-68314-779-4
Library of Congress Catalog Card Number: 2019931582

Bible versions used:
Scripture References are taken from the Holy Bible, New International Version®, NIV®. Copyright © 1973, 1978, 1984, 2011 by Biblica, Inc.™ Used by permission of Zondervan. All rights reserved worldwide. www.zondervan.com

Scripture quotations marked "ESV" are taken from The Holy Bible: English Standard Version, copyright © 2001, Wheaton: Good News Publishers. Used by permission. All rights reserved.

Permissions:
Excerpts from *Jesus Christ, Disciplemaker*, by Bill Hull, copyright © 1984, 2004. Used by permission of Baker Books, a division of Baker Publishing Group.

Dietrich Bonhoeffer, *The Cost of Discipleship*, SCM Translation 1948, 1959 © SCM Press. Used by permission of Hymns Ancient & Modern Ltd. rights@hymnsam.co.uk

Excerpt from *Same Kind of Different as Me*, by Ron Hall and Denver Moore. Copyright © 2006 Ron Hull. Used with permission of Thomas Nelson, a division of HarperCollins Publishers.

Thru the Bible with J. Vernon McGee: Volume IV Matthew–Romans. Copyright © 1983 by J. Vernon McGee. Used with permission of Thomas Nelson, a division of HarperCollins Publishers.

Taking Back Your Faith from The American Dream, by David Platt, Copyright © 2010 by David Platt. Used by permission of WaterBrook Multnomah, an imprint of Random House, a division of Penguin Random House LLC. All rights reserved.

Excerpt from *The Radical Cross: Living the Passion of Christ*, by A.W. Tozer. Copyright © 2005, 2009 by Moody Bible Institute. Used with permission.

TABLE OF CONTENTS

Introduction 11

Part 1 (Group Study) The Call: Becoming a Disciple 15

    Week 1: The Call: Becoming a Disciple 17

    Week 2: Grace 29

    Week 3: The Word of God 36

    Week 4: Prayer 43

    Week 5: The Fellowship of Believers 51

    Week 6: Witnessing 59

Part 2: The Commission: Understanding Discipleship 67

    Week 7: The Great Commission 69

    Week 8: Obedience 75

    Week 9: Commitment vs. Tradition 83

Part 3: The Charge: Practicing Discipleship

   Jesus and the Twelve: The Original Small Group 95

   Week 10: Spreading the Good News 97

   Week 11: Abandoning All for the Gospel 109

   Week 12: Go, Be Like Me 121

   Week 13: Go a New Way 131

   Week 14: Remain in Me 141

Part 4: Old Testament Example of Discipleship 149

   Week 15: Elijah Disciples Elisha 151

Part 5: A Testimony of Discipleship 163

   Week 16: Friendship to Discipleship 165

INTRODUCTION

Hi there. I'm Ellie from Kracker Springs Farm in Shelby, Alabama. When my pastor, David Warren at South Shelby Baptist Church, asked me to write a Bible study on discipleship, it took about ten minutes for me to realize I was in over my head. Not with the content, lessons, or plan, but rather with the dawning realization of what discipleship looked like in my own life. Who had I discipled? Who was I discipling? What kind of disciple was I? Who was discipling me? Who had discipled me in the past?

For years I had considered discipleship a way to become a better Christian or a better church member. But as I considered these questions, I realized discipleship is learning to become more obedient to God and His Word. Before long, I also realized I am weak, I am lacking, I don't have it all together, and I certainly don't have all the answers. The more I learned, the more I realized I don't know. I had to trust and seek God, to let go of my will and trust God's will instead.

As I considered what discipleship looked like in my own life, I realized that God had given me some amazing people to teach me, love me, and nurture me in my faith in Christ—people who have set before me steadfast examples of living out the gospel. The first who came to mind was my mother, Annette Martin. She's a true picture of the Proverbs 31 woman: wise in decisions and diligent in all tasks, while shrewdly and lovingly managing a home of hospitality. She has a sincere heart for God. Some great discipleship memories of my childhood include my mother rising early each day to study her Sunday school lesson and pray (she taught third, fourth, and fifth graders or some variation of that age group for nearly forty years). When I was growing up, she perpetually redirected me with the question, "Is that the Christian attitude?" My mother is a living picture of forgiveness. I have watched her walk that road many times. We sang hymns together. Our favorite was "Because He Lives," and we often sang it on the way home from gymnastics. As a child, I have memories of my mother also faithfully serving in other areas in our church, and she still does. What stands out to me is not how busy she was and is in church but her ability to have the right attitude. She has never kept busy merely for the sake of busyness but always to encourage others to share in God's work and grow in their own faith. That's what makes her a disciple-maker.

When I was in my twenties, God sent a new pastor and his wife to First Baptist Church of Shelby. They had an enormous impact in my life, especially the early years of married life and motherhood. Tom and Susan Minor greatly invested themselves in me, in my husband, Brad, and in our children. Brother Tom baptized all four of us, taught us, loved us, encouraged us, and shepherded us through life during his tenure as our pastor. Many years back, he encouraged and trusted me to teach Sunday school to the adults of my age. Ms. Susan also served, taught, and loved us, teaching us to grow in our faith individually and as a family.

My current pastor, David Warren, has been a disciple-maker in my life as well. He encourages me to use the spiritual gifts God has given me and allows me to exercise those gifts in our local assembly, from writing Bible studies to speaking and teaching in small groups, as well as sharing before our congregation. He is always available to answer my questions and encourage me to continue in the faith.

Tom, Susan, and David faithfully sat down with me to explain Scripture, answer questions, pray with me and for me, and provide guidance as I used my spiritual gifts.

In the midst of my challenge to become a better and more prolific disciple-maker, I discovered I was already making disciples. My favorite discipleship story is about my children. When Brad and I first learned we would be parents, everything was wrong. It was the wrong way and the wrong time, and we were not ready. Since I'd been raised in a Christian home under my mother's example of motherhood, I immediately knew I needed to surrender my life to Christ, not just believe He was who He said He was. I knew I had a great responsibility to raise this child to know Christ and to serve Him because his eternity depended on it. Brad quickly realized the same and became the spiritual leader of our new lives, as Christ intended him to be. Eventually, after encouragement from Ms. Susan, I committed to reading God's Word, studying it, and learning from it. Soon I began to love it.

Since my son, Grayson, was born, this urgency of great responsibility to raise him to know Christ has not left me. I feel the same way in raising my daughter, Hannah Kate. Neither our home nor our examples have been perfect, nor will they ever be. Nonetheless, we prayerfully and intentionally model and teach our children to grow in their faith and to serve and love others.

I have tried to instill into our children my passion for God and His Word. As I have watched and prayed, I have seen Grayson, twenty-one, and Hannah Kate, eighteen, grow in their faith. And they continue to do so. Grayson enrolled in a ministry school of pastoral leadership upon high school graduation, and then served at a church in Tokyo, Japan, for a six-month internship program. There, he worked with students and conducted street ministry. This internship helped him discern that God's plan was for him to minister here in the States rather than abroad. Hannah Kate is active in AcTeens and the church youth group. She is trying to discern God's long-term plan for her. Over her teenage years, she has built relationships with younger kiddos in our church. I pray she will continue this pattern of discipleship throughout her life.

We have discovered the power of prayer in discipleship. Three specific prayers I have prayed over my children:

- That they would "grow in the grace and knowledge of our Lord and Savior Jesus Christ" (2 Peter 3:18).
- That God would plant their feet firmly on the Rock, Jesus Christ, a firm and secure foundation.
- That God would surround them with a core group of Christian friends.

Another example of discipleship is the relationship God established between Christy Mooney and me. God brought this beautiful, sweet soul into my life about eight years ago when she first visited our church. She started coming to my Sunday school class and then got involved in church activities and outings. This example of discipleship is not one of overcoming all obstacles to lead one to grow in her faith. Rather, she made it easy. Eager to learn and grow, Christy is an easy person to love. If you knew her, you would love her too. She has become my bestie, my soul sister, a true friend who loves at all times. She wrote our story of discipleship, and you'll find it at the end of this book in Part 5: A Testimony of Discipleship.

As for me, I have taught a Bible fellowship (Sunday school) class for seventeen years. I love to encourage others to read and study God's Word and pray. I taught American and world history classes at Shelby County High School, my alma mater, in Columbiana, Alabama, for thirteen years. I still teach, but I am currently an Academic Interventionist. This is my local mission field (for now, anyway). I'd never planned to write a book. I made plans for my life, but God did too! Proverbs 16:9 says, "In their hearts humans plan their course, but the LORD establishes their steps." God used my pastor to encourage and prompt me to write this Bible study, *Be a Disciple, Make a Disciple*.

I wonder what plan God has for you. Do you know it? Have you sought Him to help you determine His path for you? I do know part of His plan for you because it's the same for me and for all of His own: to be a disciple and to make disciples of others. A disciple is simply a follower of Jesus Christ. It's simple but not easy. Nor is it easy to make disciples, which is to practice discipleship. Discipleship is the process of investing our lives into the lives of others. It is sharing our testimonies—our faith, struggles, and victories—with others to encourage and help them as they run with perseverance the race marked out for them in Christ (Hebrews 12:1).

This Bible study, *Be a Disciple, Make a Disciple*, will help you understand what a disciple is. It will also guide you as you grow and mature as a disciple of Christ and teach you why and how disciples make other disciples. Working through this study will encourage and challenge you to be a disciple and make disciples. It will help equip you with material to share, discuss, and learn as you share life with others who are eager to grow in their relationship with Christ. *Be a Disciple, Make a Disciple* is a five-part Bible study and includes both group and individual study. Parts 1, 2, and 3 should be completed with a group of no more than twelve, and parts 4 and 5 should be completed individually.

This study focuses on the importance of discipling others and using Jesus's teachings to the Twelve as the model for today. Why develop a new method or program when the original plan is gold? This isn't anything new, nor is it hard. However, it requires obedience to the call every believer receives upon salvation: follow Christ and lead others to do the same. Be a disciple and make a disciple.

For this Bible study to succeed, it should be implemented as intended. It should not become some rote, mundane, run-of-the-mill group lecture for weeks or months on end. The Bible study is designed for a group of no more than thirteen: a leader and twelve students who meet for fourteen weeks (with two weeks set aside at the end for individual study). The leader is a facilitator who has already completed the study and guides the group in discussion of the Scriptures and questions while managing the time.

Why no more than twelve students? That was the original model: Jesus and the Twelve. Jesus tasked the Twelve with making disciples on their own—taking the gospel to the world—when He said, "You will be my witnesses in Jerusalem, and in all Judea and Samaria, and to the ends of the earth" (Acts 1:8). When the study has been completed, those in the group should seek believers to disciple. Or, even more ideally, they should seek the lost and make a convert to disciple. Then each should facilitate their own study with as many as are willing, up to twelve. Occasionally a student might wish to go through the study a second time before leading others. The idea is to use this study, full of Scriptures and other authors' commentaries, to have a set time of sitting down with other believers to discuss and learn God's Word in order to "grow in the grace and knowledge of our Lord and Savior Jesus Christ" (2 Peter 3:18). This study should teach you, help you, and encourage you and your students to put that knowledge and grace into practice and see the change that obedience to Christ brings. This is discipleship.

I am excited, amazed, and in awe of what God is doing in my life, others' lives, and the life of my church. It is true, you know—the Word of God is true, and it is truth. The truth of the Word provides us with promise after promise of God's love for us, His forgiveness, mercy, and grace. The truth of the Word also commands us to love others, serve others—and make disciples. Yet many believers neglect this aspect of faith, believing they can't, or they aren't qualified, or they don't know enough to disciple others. That is true; we can't on our own, out of our own strength and abilities. Rather, Christ and the Holy Spirit work in and through us, equipping us for the calling placed on our lives as believers.

So, go and make disciples. "This is to my Father's glory, that you bear much fruit, showing yourselves to be my disciples" (John 15:8).

We cannot disciple others alone, and we cannot make disciples in our abilities and knowledge. John also said in John 15:5, "I am the vine; you are the branches. If you remain in me and I in you, you will bear much fruit; apart from me you can do nothing."

All glory and honor to Him, our God and our Savior, Jesus Christ.

PART 1 (GROUP STUDY)

ఴ

THE CALL:
BECOMING A DISCIPLE

*I don't think that you will ever be clean before God if
you don't study the Word of God. I believe that the people
who are really dangerous are the ones who are as active as
termites in our churches but who are reluctant to study the
Word of God. I consider them the most dangerous element
against the Word of God and the cause of Christ in the
world. My friend, we need to study the Word of God and
apply it to our lives.[1]*

WEEK 1

ജ

THE CALL:
BECOMING A DISCIPLE

1. Write out your definition of a disciple. Feel free to Google.

2. Based on the definition of disciple, describe (in your own words) the purpose, disciplines, and actions of a disciple of Jesus Christ.

Look up the following Scriptures and write out each verse.

John 8:31:

John 13:35:

3. Circle the current evidences in your life that prove you are a disciple of Christ (and/or write in your own).

* Desire to read and study the Bible
* Love for others
* Spending time in prayer
* Tithing
* Faithful use of spiritual gifts
* Service in the local church
* Obedience to the teachings of Christ
* Witnessing to others
* Willingness to be held accountable
* Having a mentor

_____

_____

4. Write out your definition of discipleship. Again, feel free to Google.

Based on the definition of discipleship, describe (in your own words) the purpose, practices, and actions of discipleship for Jesus Christ.

Look up the following verses and write out each one.

---

2 Timothy 2:2:

John 13:15–17:

5. Circle the current evidences in your life that prove you are a disciple-maker (and/or write in your own).

* Witnessing/winning converts
* Sharing your testimony of salvation
* Willingness to teach someone what you have learned
* Intentionality in spending time with one who is eager to learn and grow in Christ
* Having an accountability partner
* Praying diligently for the spiritual growth of others
* Reading and studying the Bible with someone
* Meeting with someone regularly to spend time in prayer
* Availability to mentor someone
* Leading a Bible study group

Self-assessment requires an honest examination of ourselves so we can realize exactly where we are in running "the race marked out for us" (Hebrews 12:1). We do this not only to determine where we are on this track of the Christian life, but also because running well requires self-discipline. As Paul said to the Corinthians, "Therefore I do not run like someone running aimlessly; I do not fight like a boxer beating the air. No, I strike a blow to my body and make it my slave so that after I have preached to others, I myself will not be disqualified for the prize" (1 Corinthians 9:26–27).

The self-assessment will probably expose a key weakness in our walk with Christ as a disciple and/or in making disciples. Discipleship is not easy. In fact, Jesus Himself said, "But small is the gate and narrow the road that leads to life, and only a few find it" (Matthew 7:14). Taking an honest look at where we are and discovering it is not where we need to be is not necessarily the problem. The problems arise when we refuse to find out, or when we know but do nothing to change. The following study of Jesus and His model of the twelve disciples should teach and encourage every Christian to be a disciple and to make disciples.

Born Again

The hallmark verse of Christianity is John 3:16: "For God so loved the world that he gave his one and only Son, that whoever believes in him shall not perish but have eternal life."

Read John 3:16 in the context of which it was written: John 3:1–21.

Describe the exchange between Nicodemus and Jesus.

What biblical truth does Jesus share with Nicodemus? See also 2 Corinthians 5:17, John 1:12–13, and Romans 8:1–2.

Salvation (being born again) comes when we surrender our will to the authority of Christ. Believing is trusting in Jesus to make us new, as He said He would, trusting that His forgiveness is complete, trusting that His Holy Spirit lives within us and seals our spirit. It also means trusting that He has gifted us and equipped us for the call, trusting that His grace is sufficient, and, yes, trusting that we will live in heaven for eternity. Salvation is so much more than merely going to heaven. Salvation changes us, makes us a new creature in the here and now, not just in eternity.

If you have never made the decision to follow Christ, never asked to be born again in Him, today is the day. Second Corinthians 6:2 says, "I tell you, now is the time of God's favor, now is the day of salvation." It starts with prayer to God our Father, confessing that you are a sinner and trusting that His blood, shed on the cross, cleanses you from sin and makes you new in Him. It's crying out to Him to be saved, and He will save you.

Born Again, a New Person. But What Now?

After salvation, we begin to follow. It's simple (the gospel: John 3:16), but it's not easy. John 3:16 is the "salt" of the gospel. However, it does not convey the complete picture of living as a believer. There is more to being a follower of Christ than believing He is who He says He is. We are also called to be both salt and light.

Matthew 5:13 tells us we are the salt of the earth. The properties of salt are undeniable. Salt wakes up the flavor; it's savory and creates thirst. Salt is a preservative, slowing the decaying process. We flavor those around us with God's love, causing others to thirst for and savor Christ and to desire a deeper relationship with Him. Believing in Jesus preserves us, but not only for heaven. It also preserves us here and now while we live out our mission of kingdom work, which is discipleship of others.

Jesus also said, "You are the light of the world" (Matthew 5:14). Light dispels darkness, exposes evil deeds, and gives us access and ability to walk the narrow path, to run the race marked out for the believer. The light in the believer is Jesus Christ; it is Jesus who not only enables us to see, but His light brings warmth and growth. The growth of Jesus Christ within us is cultivated when we die to self. Luke 9:23 illuminates the complete picture of the gospel of Jesus.

Write out Luke 9:23.

This verse communicates a three-part message: come, die, and then live. Go back and underline each of these three parts.

Look at the context in which this message was written in both Luke 9:1–25 and Matthew 16:1–26. (Both Luke and Matthew write an account of these events.) Describe the events that recently and immediately precede Jesus's teaching to the disciples in Luke 9:23–24 and Matthew 16:24–25.

What biblical truth is Jesus explaining to the disciples in Luke 9:23? See also Luke 9:24–25, 1 Corinthians 6:19–20, John 12:24–26, and Galatians 2:20.

This is the "not easy" part. Being a disciple is costly. Bill Hull, author of *Jesus Christ: Disciplemaker*, says, "Salvation itself costs us nothing, but discipleship will cost us everything."[2]

Read Luke 14:25–35. To whom was this addressed?

Was this teaching lenient or restrictive?

Was it arbitrary, optional, or mandatory?

Why would lenient or arbitrary teaching be dangerous for the Christian?

Dietrich Bonhoeffer, author of *The Cost of Discipleship*, explains this "not easy" part as follows:

> If our Christianity has ceased to be serious about discipleship, if we have watered down the gospel into emotional uplift which makes no costly demands and which fails to distinguish between natural and Christian existence, then we cannot help regarding the cross as an ordinary everyday calamity, as one of the trials and tribulations of life. We have then forgotten that the cross means rejection and shame as well as suffering . . . But this notion has ceased to be intelligible to a Christianity which can no longer see any difference

between an ordinary human life and a life committed to Christ. The cross means sharing the suffering of Christ to the last and to the fullest. Only a man thus totally committed in discipleship can experience the meaning of the cross. The cross is there, right from the beginning, he has only got to pick it up: there is no need for him to go out and look for a cross for himself, no need for him deliberately to run after suffering. Jesus says that every Christian has his own cross waiting for him, a cross destined and appointed by God. Each must endure his allotted share of suffering and rejection. But each has a different share: some God deems worthy of the highest form of suffering, and gives them the grace of martyrdom, while others he does not allow to be tempted above that which they are able to bear. But it is the one and the same cross in every case.

The cross is laid on every Christian. The first Christ-suffering which every man must experience is the call to abandon the attachments of this world. It is that dying of the old man which is the result of his encounter with Christ. As we embark upon discipleship we surrender ourselves to Christ in union with his death—we give over our lives to death. Thus it begins; the cross is not the terrible end to an otherwise God-fearing and happy life, but it meets us at the beginning of our communion with Christ. When Christ calls a man, he bids him come and die.[3]

Dying to live, being born again, is like a planted seed growing into a fruitful tree. Even Jesus said of Himself, "Very truly I tell you, unless a kernel of wheat falls to the ground and dies, it remains only a single seed. But if it dies, it produces many seeds" (John 12:24).

He continued teaching the disciples what it meant to follow, saying, "Anyone who loves their life will lose it, while anyone who hates their life in this world will keep it for eternal life" (John 12:25). Our lives are worth far more when we die to self and live for Christ.

> Take, for instance, the iron bar. A picture in a magazine shows a plain bar of iron worth $5.00. If the same iron bar were made into horseshoes, it would be worth $10.50. Fashioned into needles it would be worth $5,000, and into balance springs for watches it would actually be worth $250,000.
>
> The secret is in how it is used. So, too, human beings. The Master Fashioner of lives can transform an individual into a valuable instrument of usefulness. See what giants of usefulness Jesus made of eleven disciples.[4]

What do Luke 9:23, Luke 14:25–35, and John 12:23–26 mean to you? How have you applied this teaching to your life?

The passages are decisive and demanding. They contain difficult principles, which is why Jesus emphasized counting the cost of becoming a disciple. In explaining Himself, He said, "Suppose one of you wants to build a tower. Won't you first sit down and estimate the cost to see if he has enough money to complete it?" (Luke 14:28). The traditional gospel message has been John 3:16—just believe—while leaving off

Luke 9:23—the cost of following. Such has resulted in an ineffective local church half full of members who treat it like a social club.

David Platt, former President of the International Mission Board and author of several books, including *Radical: Taking Back Your Faith from the American Dream*, delves into this topic unapologetically. Platt concludes:

> This sounds a lot different than "Admit, believe, confess, and pray a prayer after me." And that's not all. Consider Mark 10, another time a potential follower showed up. Here is a guy who was young, rich, intelligent, and influential. He was a prime prospect, to say the least. Not only that, but he was eager and ready to go. He came running up to Jesus, bowed at his feet, and said, "What must I do to inherit eternal life?" (Mark 10:17).
>
> If we were in Jesus' shoes, we probably would be thinking this is our chance. A simple "Pray this prayer, sign this card, bow your head, and repeat after me" and this guy is in. Then think about what a guy like this with all his influence and prestige can do. We can get him on the circuit. He can start sharing his testimony, signing books, raising money for the cause. This one is a no-brainer—we have to get him in.
>
> Unfortunately, Jesus didn't have the personal evangelism books we have today that tell us how to draw the net and close the sale. Instead Jesus told him one thing: "Go, sell everything you have and give to the poor, and you will have treasure in heaven. Then come, follow me" (Mark 10:21).

What was he thinking? Jesus had committed the classic blunder of letting the big fish get away. The cost was too high.

Yet the kind of abandonment Jesus asked of the rich young man is at the core of Jesus' invitation throughout the Gospels. Even his simple call in Matthew 4 to his disciples—"Follow me"—contained radical implications for their lives. Jesus was calling them to abandon their comforts, all that was familiar to them and natural for them.

He was calling them to abandon their careers. They were reorienting their entire life's work around discipleship to Jesus. Their plans and dreams were now being swallowed up in his.

Jesus was calling them to abandon their possessions. "Drop your nets and your trades as successful fishermen," he was saying in effect.

Jesus was calling them to abandon their family and their friends. When James and John left their father, we see Jesus' words in Luke 14 come alive.

Ultimately, Jesus was calling them to abandon themselves. They were leaving certainty for uncertainty, safety for danger, self-preservation for self-denunciation. In a world that prizes promoting oneself, they were following a teacher who told them to crucify themselves. And history tells us the result. Almost all of them would lose their lives because they responded to his invitation.[5]

Reflect on Platt's assessment of traditional church lingo of witnessing compared to the passages of Scriptures discussed in this week's study.

What do you think? Has the church waded into a watered-down version of the gospel to make it easier for the one witnessing and the one being witnessed to? If so or if not, please explain.

Scripture of Challenge/Encouragement:

> Therefore, my dear friends, as you have always obeyed—not only in my presence, but now much more in my absence—continue to work out your salvation with fear and trembling, for it is God who works in you to will and to act in order to fulfill his good purpose. Do everything without grumbling or arguing, so that you may become blameless and pure, "children of God without fault in a warped and crooked generation." Then you will shine among them like stars in the sky as you hold firmly to the word of life. And then I will be able to boast on the day of Christ that I did not run or labor in vain. (Philippians 2:12–16)

Prayer: Meditate on the passage from Philippians, then write out a prayer asking God to speak to you and help you fulfill these verses in your life.

WEEK 2

ɞ

GRACE

Last week we talked about becoming a disciple. Since your last meeting, what insights did God give you about this topic?

How is it possible to take up our cross and follow Jesus? Matthew 19:26 says, "With man this is impossible, but with God all things are possible." Jesus didn't mean for us to take this verse out of context and apply it like a blanket wherever we want. Look up Matthew 19:16–27. In what context did Jesus speak Matthew 19:26?

Taking up our cross is possible because of grace, God's grace. The apostle Paul grew to understand this truth and apply it to his life as a believer and disciple-maker. When Saul became Paul by grace through faith, his life did not become one of ease without sacrifice. In fact, his life became the opposite. Paul wrote to the Corinthians of his hardships and struggles, trying to explain to them that God's grace strengthened him and enabled him to boast in Christ's victory in his life.

Second Corinthians 11:23–33 says:

> Are they servants of Christ? (I am out of my mind to talk like this.) I am more. I have worked much harder, been in prison more frequently, been flogged more severely, and been exposed to death again and again. Five times I received from the Jews the forty lashes minus one. Three times I was beaten with rods, once I was pelted with stones, three times I was shipwrecked, I spent a night and a day in the open sea, I have been constantly on the move. I have been in danger from rivers, in danger from bandits, in danger from my fellow Jews, in danger from Gentiles; in danger in the city, in danger in the country, in danger at sea; and in danger from false believers. I have labored and toiled and have often gone without sleep; I have known hunger and thirst and have often gone without food; I have been cold and naked. Besides everything else, I face daily the pressure of my concern for all the churches. Who is weak, and I do not feel weak? Who is led into sin, and I do not inwardly burn? If I must boast, I will boast of the things that show my weakness. The God and Father of the Lord Jesus, who is to be praised forever, knows that I am not lying. In Damascus the governor under King Aretas had the city of the Damascenes guarded in order to arrest me. But I was lowered in a basket from a window in the wall and slipped through his hands.

In the context of those verses, Paul wrote about the sufficiency of grace. God's grace is sufficient and free; it's just not cheap. Look up 2 Corinthians 12:9–10. What do these verses teach you about God's grace?

Freedom isn't free, and grace isn't cheap. God's grace cost Him His Son, yet the Church has adopted cheap grace. What is cheap grace? Bonhoeffer explained it best in his book, *The Cost of Discipleship*:

> Cheap grace is the preaching of forgiveness without requiring repentance, baptism without church discipline, Communion without confession, absolution without personal confession. Cheap grace is grace without discipleship, grace without the cross, grace without Jesus Christ, living and incarnate.[6]

> I can go and sin as much as I like and rely on this grace to forgive me, for after all the world is justified in principle by grace. I can therefore cling to my bourgeois [middle-class] secular existence, and remain as I was before, but with the added assurance that the grace of God will cover me. It is under the influence of this kind of "grace" that the world has been made "Christian," but at the cost of secularizing the Christian religion as never before. The antithesis between the Christian life and the life of bourgeois respectability is at an end. The Christian life comes to mean nothing more than living in the world and as the world, in being no different from the world, in fact, in being prohibited from being different from the world for the sake of grace. The upshot of it all is that my only duty as a Christian is to leave the world for an hour or so on a Sunday morning and go to church to be assured that my sins are all forgiven.

I need no longer try to follow Christ, for cheap grace, the bitterest foe of discipleship, which true discipleship must loathe and detest, has freed me from that.[7]

Do you see this adoption and application of cheap grace in your own life? In the local church? Why or why not?

You say, "But I thought God's grace was free and unlimited. It's God's gift to me. I can do nothing to earn it. God gives it freely because He loves me, loves us all more than we can comprehend." We find this truth in Ephesians 2:4–5, 7–9, and John 1:16–17. What do these verses teach you about grace?

Grace costs you nothing. However, it cost the Father His one and only Son, Jesus Christ, by way of a cruel cross of suffering. We can do nothing to earn grace. God freely gives it. But when we receive grace, our hearts are forever changed. A new creature is born; thus we live a new life in Christ Jesus. The prophet Isaiah prophesied that Christ would suffer God's wrath for you and me. Read Isaiah 53:4–7, 10–12. What do these verses prophesy about the coming Christ?

Therefore, grace received unto salvation must be costly grace. Again, Bonhoeffer explains it best.

Costly grace is the treasure hidden in the field; for the sake of it man will gladly go and sell all that he has. It is the pearl of great price to buy which the merchant will sell all his goods. It is the kingly rule of Christ, for whose sake a man will pluck out the eye which causes him to stumble; it is the call of Jesus Christ at which the disciple leaves his nets and follows him.

Costly grace is the gospel which must be *sought* again and again, the gift which must be *asked* for, the door at which a man must *knock*.

Such grace is *costly* because it calls us to follow, and it is *grace* because it calls us to follow *Jesus Christ*. It is costly because it costs a man his life, and it is grace because it gives a man the only true life. It is costly because it condemns sin, and grace because it justifies the sinner. Above all, it is *costly* because it cost God the life of his Son: "ye were bought at a price," and what has cost God much cannot be cheap for us. Above all, it is *grace* because God did not reckon his Son too dear a price to pay for our life but delivered him up for us. Costly grace is the Incarnation of God.

Costly grace is the sanctuary of God; it has to be protected from the world and not thrown to the dogs. It is therefore the living word, the Word of God, which he speaks as it pleases him. Costly grace confronts us as a gracious call to follow Jesus, it comes as a word of forgiveness to the broken spirit and the contrite heart. Grace is costly because it compels a man to submit to the yoke of Christ and follow him; it is grace because Jesus says: "My yoke is easy and my burden is light."[8]

Therefore, our purpose in this study is to answer the call to true discipleship. First, we must understand how to become a disciple of Jesus Christ, a true follower, making sure we undertake the disciplines of a follower (Bible study, prayer, fasting, worship, witnessing, and fellowship). Second, we must fulfill the command to make disciples by passing on our knowledge, experiences, trials, shortcomings, victories, challenges, and praises to someone else through intentional, committed, loving relationship. It's the multiply effect. Our reason for doing so lies in our passion to rescue the local church (congregations of believers) from the mundane, empty, nonproducing tradition of organized religion.

Scripture of Challenge/Encouragement:

> But he said to me, "My grace is sufficient for you, for my power is made perfect in weakness." Therefore I will boast all the more gladly about my weaknesses, so that Christ's power may rest on me. That is why, for Christ's sake, I delight in weaknesses, in insults, in hardships, in persecutions, in difficulties. For when I am weak, then I am strong. (2 Corinthians 12:9–10)

Prayer: Meditate on the passage from Corinthians, then write out a prayer asking God for His grace to enable you to live victoriously in Him and fulfill the call to make disciples.

ᛥ

THE WORD OF GOD

Last week we talked about grace. Since your last meeting, what insights did God give you about this topic?

This study should be a how-to for the follower of Christ, teaching us what it means to live under costly grace. In his book *Jesus Christ: Disciplemaker*, Bill Hull identifies four fundamentals for the disciple of Christ. Disciples should be established "in the Word of God, prayer, fellowship and witnessing."[9] An examination of each of these four fundamentals in Scripture will reveal the necessity for the true disciple to be established in such spiritual disciplines.

First, let's examine the Christian's responsibility to read, study, and know the Word of God. Why does a follower of Jesus have a responsibility, even a need, to read, study, and know the Word of God?

Would you say you have a desire to read, study, and know God's Word?

On average, how much time do you spend reading and studying the Bible per day?

Not at all   10 minutes   20 minutes   30 minutes   60 minutes

If you usually do not read and study God's Word, what hinders you?

Jesus and the disciples were well-versed in Old Testament Scripture, as we can see by the number of times they quoted God's Word. Jesus quoted the book of Deuteronomy as He resisted temptation from the devil while in the desert (Matthew 4:4–10). Throughout His earthly ministry, Jesus continued to quote from the Old Testament throughout the four gospels.

The book of Acts also provides great evidence of Peter and Paul's knowledge and use of Scripture. Even the early believers "devoted themselves to the apostles' teaching and to fellowship, to the breaking of bread and to prayer" (Acts 2:42). Yet most churchgoers do not have a developed practice of reading and studying the Bible. The following online article of a recent survey supplies sufficient evidence for such a statement.

The Bible—Helpful, but Not Read Much

> *"Among Americans: How much of the Bible have you personally read?"*
>
> The Bible may be a source of wisdom for many Americans but most don't read it for themselves, a new survey shows. More than half have read little or none of it,

reports LifeWay Research. "Even among worship attendees less than half read the Bible daily," said Scott McConnell, executive director of the evangelical research firm based in Nashville, Tenn. "The only time most Americans hear from the Bible is when someone else is reading it."

The survey of 1,000 people found disparate approaches to the Christian Scriptures. For instance, Northeasterners are less likely to give it a look than people in other regions. And men are less inclined than women to pick it up.

"Among Americans: Which of the following describe the Bible?"

One in 5 Americans have read the entire Bible at least once— including 9 percent who've read it through multiple times. Just over half (53 percent) have read relatively little of it, and 1 in 10 haven't read it at all.

Among those who read at least a few sentences of the Bible, slightly more than a fifth of Americans (22 percent) read a little Scripture each day, taking a systematic approach. About a quarter (27 percent) read parts others have suggested, and 16 percent look up portions to help others. Almost one-fifth (19 percent) reread their favorite passages.

Americans with evangelical beliefs are far more likely to read a little of the Bible each day than those without such beliefs (49 percent vs. 16 percent). Protestants are more likely to read the book each day than Catholics (36 percent and 17 percent, respectively).

Researchers found that Americans tend to view the Bible positively, with half (52 percent) saying it is a good source for morals. More than a third say it is helpful today (37 percent), true (36 percent) or life-changing (35 percent). And far fewer say it is outdated (14 percent), bigoted (8 percent) or harmful (7 percent).

"Among Americans: Why have you not read the Bible more?"

- Don't prioritize it (27 percent).
- Don't have time (15 percent).
- Have read it enough (13 percent).
- Disagree with what it says (10 percent).
- Don't read books (9 percent).
- Don't see how it relates to them (9 percent).
- Don't have one (6 percent).

The survey of 1,000 people, drawn from a panel designed to be representative of the U.S. population, was conducted Sept. 27 Oct. 1, 2016, and had an overall margin of error of plus or minus 3.1 percentage points.[10]

This survey reveals a critical issue for the Church, especially the local church: many people who claim Christ have no knowledge or interest in Him. All the while, "Christians" *wander* aimlessly through life and then *wonder* why their "Christian life" is empty, devoid of power, and lifeless. They experience no growth, no victory, even though a Sunday morning sermon told them that Jesus gives life more abundantly.

God's Word shows us why Bible reading, study, and knowledge are vital for the follower of Christ. The prophet Isaiah exclaimed, "The grass withers and the flowers fall, because the breath of the LORD blows on them. Surely the people are grass. The grass withers and the flowers fall, but the word of our God endures forever" (Isaiah 40:7–8).

Look up the following verses that show how vital the Bible is to the Christ-follower. Write out the verses in the space provided.

Hebrews 4:12:

2 Timothy 3:16–17:

2 Peter 1:3–4, 12–15, 19–21:

What do those verses teach you?

How do those verses encourage you and/or convict you?

People give an array of excuses for lack of or even nonexistent Bible reading and studying. Bill Hull says, "The Bible is a frustrating, guilt-producing document if the reader does not practice its principles."[11] Do you agree or disagree with this quote and why?

Hull's statement is accurate. The reason lies at the core of man: the heart. The heart is the soul of man, the whole of man—the seat of human emotion and will. Matthew 6:21 confirms this, stating, "For where your treasure is, there your heart will be also." A myriad of "things" compete for the throne of the heart, but each of these falls into one of two categories: self or the Holy Spirit. A.W. Tozer explains it in the following words:

> In every Christian's heart there is a cross and a throne, and the Christian is on the throne till he puts himself on the cross; if he refuses the cross, he remains on the throne. Perhaps this is at the bottom of the backsliding and worldliness among gospel believers today. We want to be saved, but we insist that Christ do all the dying. No cross for us, no dethronement, no dying. We remain king within the little kingdom of Man's soul and wear our tinsel crown with all the pride of a Caesar, but we doom ourselves to shadows and weakness and spiritual sterility.[12]

Look up Proverbs 4:23 and write it out.

Does this verse support or refute Tozer's statement? How?

The prophet Jeremiah certainly knew the danger of the human heart as he wrote the words God spoke to him: "The heart is deceitful above all things and beyond cure. Who can understand it?" (Jeremiah 17:9). This is why Jesus said the greatest command is to love the Lord your God with all your heart (Matthew 22:37). Certainly part of loving the Lord our God with all our hearts means knowing His written Word. The apostle John, the closest to Jesus, began his gospel with the proclamation, "In the beginning was the Word, and the

Word was with God, and the Word was God" (John 1:1). John continued in verse 14, stating, "The Word became flesh and made his dwelling among us."

What do you learn about Jesus Christ from the above verses?

Do these verses compel you to a lifelong practice of reading, studying, and learning God's Word?

Jesus cautioned us against having knowledge of the Word but not letting it change our hearts, not applying it to our lives. He was quick to condemn the Pharisees for knowledge without application.

Look up John 5:37–47. What do these verses say about having knowledge that we don't apply to our hearts?

This is why Paul wrote to the Colossians: "Let the message of Christ dwell among you richly as you teach and admonish one another with all wisdom through psalms, hymns, and songs from the Spirit, singing to God with gratitude in your hearts" (Colossians 3:16). Even so, John 1:1 and 14 teach us this: the Bible, God's Word, is your tangible Jesus. If we have no desire to read and study His Word, we have no desire to be with Christ, no desire to know Christ. And if that's the case, we do not love the Lord our God. Look up John 14:15, 23 for additional evidence and write out each verse.

May we search the Scriptures out of obedience and prayerfully seek God to fill our hearts with a genuine desire to read, study, learn, and know God's Word.

Scripture of Challenge/Encouragement:

> Hear, O Israel: The LORD our God, the LORD is one. Love the LORD your God with all your heart and with all your soul and with all your strength. These commandments that I give you today are to be on your hearts. Impress them on your children. Talk about them when you sit at home and when you walk along the road, when you lie down and when you get up. Tie them as symbols on your hands and bind them on your foreheads. Write them on the doorframes of your houses and on your gates. (Deuteronomy 6:4–9)

Prayer: Meditate on the passage from Deuteronomy, then write out a prayer asking God to give you a passion for His Word and grace to help you share with others.

WEEK 4

ဢ

PRAYER

Last week we talked about the Word of God. Since your last meeting, what insights did God give you about this topic?

This week let's examine the spiritual discipline of prayer. Communication with God is the lifeblood for the disciple of Christ. Prayer is a holy conversation with the Father including worship, praise, adoration, thanksgiving, supplication, petition, and listening.

Why does a Christ-follower have a responsibility, even a need, to spend time in prayer?

On average, how much do you pray each day?

Not at all   10 minutes   20 minutes   30 minutes   60 minutes

Do you have a quiet place, free of distraction, where you can be alone with the Lord?

Do you struggle with spending time in conversation and listening to God? If so, explain. If not, have you ever considered praying with others, teaching them by modeling your prayer life?

Jesus practiced a strong prayer life, and He modeled and expected a strong prayer life for His disciples as well. Mark's gospel is the first to record Jesus's practice of prayer: "Very early in the morning, while it was still dark, Jesus got up, left the house and went off to a solitary place, where he prayed" (Mark 1:35). Luke, the doctor, gave particular attention to Jesus's discipline of prayer throughout his record of Jesus's earthly ministry. Luke recorded, "Jesus was baptized too. And as he was praying . . ." (Luke 3:21), "Jesus often withdrew to lonely places and prayed" (Luke 5:16), and "Jesus went out to a mountainside to pray, and spent the night praying to God" (Luke 6:12).

Dr. Luke also wrote, "Jesus told his disciples a parable to show them that they should always pray and not give up" (Luke 18:1). And Matthew, the former tax collector (another detail-oriented profession), recorded Jesus's Sermon on the Mount carefully. He noted the Lord's Prayer, which is the model prayer. Jesus devoted Himself to prayer and taught His disciples to do the same, knowing we receive all our authority and power from God. Therefore, prayer is a learned behavior. It is a discipline the disciple of Christ must practice.

Read Luke 11:1–13 and Matthew 6:5–13. What do these passages teach you regarding prayer?

This is a model of how to pray, not just a prayer to memorize. However, we can benefit from memorizing and quoting it. How is this a model of how to pray?

John, the one whom Jesus loved, observed the details of Jesus's prayers in Gethsemane the night before His crucifixion. Jesus prayed for Himself, His disciples, and all believers, as dutifully recorded in John, chapter 17.

Dr. Luke revealed the graphic anguish of soul as Christ cried out to the Father: "And being in anguish, he prayed more earnestly, and his sweat was like drops of blood falling to the ground" (Luke 22:44). Interestingly enough, Matthew recorded Jesus admonishing the disciples for their lack of prayer in Gethsemane. Look up Matthew 26:40–45. Would Jesus commend you or admonish you for your time spent in prayer?

If Jesus took time to pray and taught His disciples to pray, how much more should we? Bill Hull stated, "Jesus was teaching his men, through his own example, that prayer is foundational to ministry. Prayer and Bible study form two of four pillars of Christian life. As Jesus demonstrated both the authority of Scripture and the priority of prayer, the minds of his harried disciples were being engraved by their Master's poignant demonstration of personal devotion to his Father."[13]

In the mid-1950s, Samuel T. Scott and Robert L. Sande wrote a song titled, "Prayer is the Key to Heaven, but Faith Unlocks the Door." It implies our entry to the Father is through prayer. Prayer is communion, communication, and fellowship with the Father. Our Lord and Savior Jesus Christ made this privilege possible for believers.

Look up the following Scriptures regarding Jesus and prayer. What does each of these Scriptures in Hebrews teach us about prayer and Jesus's role in our prayers?

1. Hebrews 7:25

2. Hebrews 9:15

3. Hebrews 10:10

4. Hebrews 10:12

5. Hebrews 10:19–22

6. Hebrews 4:16

The best way to learn to pray is to read and study the Word, paying special attention to the numerous prayers of the Old Testament saints who came before us. These people were not perfect, and this makes them relatable. However, they provide perfect examples of prayer. Take a look at Solomon's prayer of dedication for the temple in 1 Kings 8:22–53. See also Nehemiah 1:4–11 (Nehemiah's prayer for Jerusalem) and Daniel 9:4–19 (Daniel's prayer for the Israelites in captivity).

Do you notice a pattern in the beginning of these prayers? What is it?

What other patterns are evident in these prayers?

On the cross Jesus cried out to God in prayer, "My God, my God, why have you forsaken me?" (Matthew 27:46). We should learn to cry out to God in prayer too. Again, Old Testament saints provide examples. The psalmist, King David, cried out to God in prayer, petitioned Him for deliverance, proclaimed His great name in prayer, and praised Him for His victories in prayer. See Psalms 18, 22, 69, 103, and 138 as evidence and for future reference when praying. How might these psalms aid you in developing your prayer life? List any other psalms you have discovered and share them with your group.

Psalms is my favorite book in the Bible. There are 150 psalms. Some are short and some are rather lengthy, but each one is a prayer or song of some sort, filled with instructional goodness. They are often the words I pray when I can't seem to find words of my own. Use the Psalms, along with these other prayers, to learn how to pray and how to pray Scripture. Let God's Word teach you, rebuke you, correct you, and train you in righteousness so that you may be thoroughly equipped for every good work (2 Timothy 3:16–17).

Scripture of Challenge/Encouragement:

> In you, LORD my God,
> I put my trust.
> I trust in you;
> do not let me be put to shame,
> nor let my enemies triumph over me.
> No one who hopes in you
> will ever be put to shame,
> but shame will come on those
> who are treacherous without cause.
> Show me your ways, LORD,
> teach me your paths.
> Guide me in your truth and teach me,
> for you are God my Savior,
> and my hope is in you all day long.
> (Psalm 25:1–5)

Prayer: Meditate on these verses from Psalm 25, then write out a prayer personalizing this psalm and making it your own.

Prayer

49

WEEK 5

 જી

THE FELLOWSHIP OF BELIEVERS

Last week we talked about prayer. Since your last meeting, what insights did God give you about this topic?

The third fundamental of discipleship is fellowship among believers. Such a practice is not mere socialization, but a time of encouragement and accountability in the spiritual disciplines.

Do you see fellowship as fundamental for the disciple? Why or why not? See Ecclesiastes 4:9–12 for further insight.

Circle the examples below that you think hinder meaningful, fulfilling, and encouraging fellowship (or add your own).

Selfishness   Immature/weak faith   Insecurity   Bad attitude
     Complainers   Time   Lack of desire   Laziness
Impatience with others   Nervous or shy   Fear

Yes, fellowship with other believers is important; it's essential to the healthy spiritual life of the disciple. However, we first must have fellowship with Christ, the author and finisher of our faith (Hebrews 12:2). Only then will our fellowship with believers be fruitful and fulfilling.

Read the following passage, and then complete the directions and questions pertaining to the passage.

That which was from the beginning, which we have heard, which we have seen with our eyes, which we have looked at and our hands have touched—this we proclaim concerning the Word of life. The life appeared; we have seen it and testify to it, and we proclaim to you the eternal life, which was with the Father and has appeared to us. We proclaim to you what we have seen and heard, so that you also may have fellowship with us. And our fellowship is with the Father and with his Son, Jesus Christ. We write this to make our joy complete. This is the message we have heard from him and declare to you: God is light; in him there is no darkness at all. If we claim to have fellowship with him yet walk in the darkness, we lie and do not live by the truth. But if we walk in the light, as he is in the light, we have fellowship with one another, and the blood of Jesus, his Son, purifies us from all sin. (1 John 1:1–7)

1. Circle each instance of the word *fellowship* in the above passage.

2. What must happen before we can have fellowship with other believers?

3. According to verse 7, how can we experience fellowship?

When the vertical relationship is vibrant (Philippians 4:13), the horizontal relationships can thrive (Proverbs 27:17). It's the connection and the intersection.

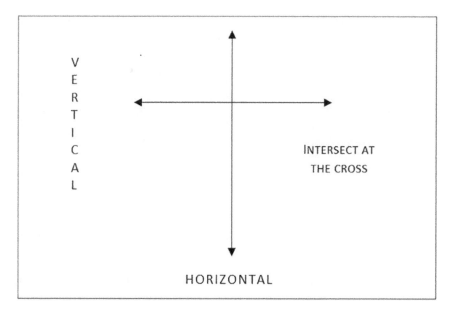

In other words, the health of our relationship with the Father determines the health of our earthly relationships. Our personal relationship with Christ enables us to have dynamic, meaningful, intimate fellowship with other believers. The early church in Acts understood this and experienced such fellowship. Read Acts 2:42–47. What does it say about the first group of believers?

Selfishness, arrogance, and jealousy found no place in their gatherings because there is no room for such in kingdom relationships and work. This doesn't mean the early church never experienced such issues, because it did (Ananias and Sapphira in Acts 5:3–11, for example). As Paul and his fellow worker established churches in Asia Minor, he wrote to them and cautioned them to avoid certain hindering behaviors. He also instructed them in godly behaviors with one another.

He urged the Ephesians (4:1–6, 12–16).
He reminded the Romans (12:9–21).
He exhorted the Corinthians (1 Corinthians 12:24–27).
He informed the Colossians (3:12–14).

From these passages, choose at least five instructions you feel are most important to forming genuine, uplifting fellowship among disciples.

1.

2.

3.

4.

5.

Which of these passages speak to you more personally about true fellowship and why?

Remember, fellowship is not surface-level greetings with a superficial, "How are you?" and answered with a masked, "Fine." Real fellowship takes place when people are open and honest, not only with each other, but also with themselves. This kind of raw experience with fellow believers exists only when we are trustworthy and caring, when we love one another as Christ commanded. Jesus said, "My command is this: Love each other as I have loved you" (John 15:12). This was Jesus's foremost teaching, and He said it is a measure of our devotion to Him. He said, "If you hold to my teaching, you are really my disciples" (John 8:31).

Read 1 John 4:7–12 and summarize:

True fellowship of believers grows out of the fertile soil of love for one another, and there, healthy relationships take root. We are meant to live in relationship with one another; life is meant to be shared, especially for the disciple. Think about it. Every earthly relationship is in some way a picture of our relationship with our Creator, the Godhead (the Father, the Son, the Holy Spirit).

Husband and wife: The Church is the bride of Christ (Isaiah 54:5 and Revelation 21:9).

Parent and child: God is our Father (Matthew 6:9 and 1 John 3:1).

Siblings/Kin: Saints from every nation (1 Corinthians 1:2 and Ephesians 2:18–19).

Friends: Our obedience to Christ makes us friends of Christ (John 15:12–15).

Mentor and mentee: The Holy Spirit lives in the believer (1 Corinthians 2:12–13).

We are to learn how best to relate to one another based on the models of relationship God provided. He set the standard, and His standard has not changed in spite of man's attempt to thwart it and/or dumb it down. We are to love one another, as Jesus repeatedly instructs us in His Word.

The writer of Hebrews encourages believers to persevere, not individually, but together. Read Hebrews 10:19–25. Notice the collective nouns/pronouns of *brothers*, *we*, and *us*. Truly, the picture he paints is one of believers walking with Christ together.

List four exhortations this passage instructs believers to follow.

1.

2.

3.

4.

This is the fellowship of disciples: holding onto the hope we profess in Christ, spurring one another on with good deeds, continuing to meet together, and encouraging one another.

Scripture of Challenge/Encouragement:

> Therefore encourage one another and build each other
> up, just as in fact you are doing. (1 Thessalonians 5:11)

Prayer: Meditate on 1 Thessalonians 5:11. Then write out a prayer thanking God for those He has placed in your life, so you can enjoy sweet fellowship that encourages you and builds your faith in Christ Jesus. Consider sending one or more of them a note of thanks for their encouragement in your life.

WEEK 6

ॐ

WITNESSING

Last week we talked about the fellowship of believers. Since your last meeting, what insights did God give you about this topic?

This week let's study witnessing as our fourth fundamental that equips the disciple to disciple others. Jesus came to tell the good news of salvation, calling sinners unto Himself and offering forgiveness of sin. Once Jesus's earthly ministry began, the first word He spoke was, "Come" (John 1:39). He quickly followed up with, "And you will see." Jesus picked up right where John the Baptist had paved His way: "A voice of one calling: 'In the wilderness prepare the way for the LORD; make straight in the desert a highway for our God'" (Isaiah 40:3). John had been preaching, "Look, the Lamb of God, who takes away the sin of the world!" (John 1:29). John the Baptist had been the faithful witness of Christ's coming and His purpose, like "the moon, the faithful witness in the sky" (Psalm 89:37). As the moon reflects the light of the sun, John the Baptist reflected the light of the Son. We are to do the same. Jesus taught just that in the Sermon on the Mount.

Read Matthew 5:14–16. What does Jesus say we are?

What does He say we should do?

How can we practice this in our day-to-day lives?

Letting your light shine before men is simply telling others who Jesus is, sharing what He has done for you, and loving them as Jesus loves you. That is witnessing. In the Gospel of Mark we learn about the healing of the demon-possessed man and Jesus's response to him when the man wanted to go with Jesus: "Jesus did not let him, but said, 'Go home to your own people and tell them how much the Lord has done for you, and how he has had mercy on you.' So the man went away and began to tell in the Decapolis [ten cities] how much Jesus had done for him. And all the people were amazed" (Mark 5:19–20).

Similarly, the Samaritan woman at the well encountered Christ. Read John 4:4–30.

What did the woman do when she learned who Jesus was?

Read John 4:39–42. What happened in Samaria as a result of this woman telling her people about Jesus and what He did for her?

We have been instructed to tell others who Jesus is and what He has done for us, just as the demon-possessed man was instructed and the woman at the well did on her own. Following the charge of the Great Commission in Matthew 28:19–20 and preceding His ascension, Jesus instructed His followers about their mission: "But you will receive power when the Holy Spirit comes on you; and you will be my witnesses in Jerusalem, and in all Judea and Samaria, and to the ends of the earth" (Acts 1:8). How does such instruction apply to us, since we don't live in Jerusalem? We are to be His witnesses in our town, in our state, in our country, even across the whole world—in "all nations." Jesus modeled this for us during His earthly ministry.

Look up Proverbs 11:30 and write it out.

Winning souls (witnessing) is simply sharing with others who Jesus Christ is and what He did for you, how He changed you on the inside and made you whole. It helps to know some witnessing Scriptures and use them to explain salvation. Below is a list of verses you can use to lead someone to salvation in Christ.

For all have sinned and fall short of the glory of God (Romans 3:23).

For the wages of sin is death, but the gift of God is eternal life in Christ Jesus our Lord (Romans 6:23).

If we confess our sins, he is faithful and just and will forgive us our sins and purify us from all unrighteousness (1 John 1:9).

For God so loved the world that he gave his one and only Son, that whoever believes in him shall not perish but have eternal life (John 3:16).

Then he said to them all: "Whoever wants to be my disciple must deny themselves and take up their cross daily and follow me" (Luke 9:23).

For it is by grace you have been saved, through faith— and this is not from yourselves, it is the gift of God—not by works, so that no one can boast (Ephesians 2:8–9).

So if the Son sets you free, you will be free indeed (John 8:36).

When witnessing, share your story of salvation. It's your testimony of Christ's power in your life. Share some or all of the verses listed above. When those you are witnessing to are ready to make the decision to follow Christ, encourage them to pray. Direct them to confess their sins, ask for forgiveness, and commit themselves to Christ, rather than to repeat after you. Nowhere in Scripture did anyone repeat someone else's salvation prayer.

We need to remember that inviting someone to church is not witnessing. It is a good thing, and we should do it, but inviting people to church is part of discipleship, not witnessing. Discipleship comes after witnessing, after one has believed and decided to follow.

A witness's walk must match their talk. Our talk must flow naturally. In other words, we should live what we say we believe. If witnessing is part of our daily lives, then our conversations and encounters in the grocery store, gas station, local chat and chew, our job, the school, and the ballpark must reflect Christ. Remember, we are the light of the world, the light that shines in the darkness. We cannot dispel darkness if we are part of the darkness.

Being a witness for Christ is telling others about Christ and showing them Christ in you and how He has transformed you. Witnessing means loving difficult people (Matthew 5:43–46), overlooking an offense (Proverbs 19:11), giving a gentle answer (Proverbs 15:1), forgiving those who wronged you (Matthew 6:14), being kind (Ephesians 4:32), working hard (Colossians 3:23–24), being faithful (Luke 16:10), expecting no praise from man (Proverbs 27:2), showing up on time (Philippians 2:3–4), admitting when you're wrong (Proverbs 28:13), and not lashing out in your anger (Ephesians 4:26).

Cursing the coach, telling off the school, badmouthing the church, or slandering your neighbor face to face or in social media posts will not win converts. Such behaviors will make witnessing much more difficult for the ones who faithfully seek to do so. In other words, "Follow God's example, therefore, as dearly loved children and walk in the way of love, just as Christ loved us and gave himself up for us as a fragrant offering and sacrifice to God" (Ephesians 5:1–2).

Scripture of Challenge/Encouragement:

> Come and listen, all you who fear God; let me tell you
> what he has done for me. (Psalm 66:16)

Prayer: Meditate on this verse from Psalm 66, then write a prayer asking God to help you share your testimony and lead others to faith in Christ. Consider writing down the names of those you need to witness to and commit to pray for them and their salvation.

PART 1 SUMMARY

In part 1, The Call: Becoming a Disciple, we have assessed ourselves in the faith and studied the fundamentals of Christian life. List the four fundamentals:

1.

2.

3.

4.

What do you feel the Holy Spirit has taught you or impressed upon you in part 1 of this Bible study?

PART 2 (GROUP STUDY)

&

THE COMMISSION: UNDERSTANDING DISCIPLESHIP

True disciplemaking is difficult because it entails change, it takes a long time, and it is hard to visualize. It is teeming with both possibilities and problems. As in the case of the disciples, who had to launch out into deep water to confirm their call, each person who decides to follow the Master must launch out in faith, taking chances and facing the challenges of building other disciples. I once read an inscription on the side of a building: "A man who sees the invisible, hears the inaudible, believes the incredible, and thinks the unthinkable." This kind of person is a disciple.[14]

ಬಿ

THE GREAT COMMISSION

Last week we talked about witnessing. Since your last meeting, what insights did God give you about this topic?

The Great Commission (Matthew 28:19–20) is the mission statement for the Church. Write it out below.

Circle the following examples of practical ways (or write in your own) in which the local church can accomplish this.

Promote and encourage discipleship

Local mission projects

Missions offerings

Get to know new people in your church

backyard Bible club

Organize mission trips, both domestic and foreign

Monetary support for missionaries

Sit with new people at fellowship meals/socials

Small groups at the church and in homes

Greet and welcome people in your church

Circle the following examples of practical ways (or write in your own) in which you can accomplish this.

Going on mission trip

Giving to mission offerings

Teaching others

Hosting a social at my house

Leading a small group

Praying for others' salvation and spiritual growth

Sponsoring a child in a foreign country

Participating in local mission projects/outreach

Exercising my spiritual gifts

Intentionally building relationships with others

The disciples fulfilled the prophecy spoken of them in Isaiah 49:6: "I will also make you a light for the Gentiles, that my salvation may reach to the ends of the earth." After the ascension, clearly the early church disciples lived out the command to make disciples: "They preached the gospel in that city [Derbe] and won a large number of disciples. Then they returned to Lystra, Iconium and Antioch, strengthening the disciples and encouraging them to remain true to the faith" (Acts 14:21–22).

The twenty-first century Church has the same Holy Spirit power and many more modern-day resources than the first century church, yet the first century church had greater success in making disciples. Why? They followed the plan Jesus gave them, and He blessed it. But the more worldly progress we've made, the more we've deviated from Jesus's plan by choosing programs, entertainment, and socials of all sorts with only surface-level encounters.

We neglect to make a connection with the lost, so they see no real commitment from the church. Therefore, they come and go as we continue to meet and plan more programs. The church then spins its wheels, attempting to reach the lost who are stuck in the mud of their sin. We must go and make disciples as Jesus taught; that is the plan. David Platt weighs in on this subject too: "We are the plan of God, and there is no Plan B."[15]

Remember, God designed us to live in relationship, and in doing so, to spread the gospel. Platt also concludes, "There is not one verse in the book of Acts where the gospel advances to the lost apart from a human agent."[16]

Again, we call God's plan the Great Commission. Matthew recorded Jesus's final teaching, saying, "Then Jesus came to them and said, 'All authority in heaven and on earth has been given to me. Therefore go and make disciples of all nations, baptizing them in the name of the Father and of the Son and of the Holy Spirit, and teaching them to obey everything I have commanded you. And surely I am with you always, to the very end of the age'" (Matthew 28:18–20).

Why did Jesus give them (us) this final instruction before He ascended to heaven?

What was the first directive in the Great Commission?

What was the second directive?

What's the third directive?

What's the fourth directive?

Then Jesus followed up His instructions with a promise. What is the promise?

The promise should sound familiar because it is similar to the ones God gave Moses (Exodus 3:12), the Israelites (Deuteronomy 31:6), Joshua (Joshua 1:5), and the Virgin Mary (Luke 1:28).

Why do you think God concluded these instructions with a promise?

Do you live as if you believe this promise is for you today? Explain.

Before we can discuss how to go and make disciples, we must get to the core of the Great Commission. At the heart of these final instructions of "go and make disciples, baptize and teach" is simple obedience. We are to obey what Jesus has commanded: to go and make disciples, baptize, and teach others to follow Him. This command doesn't make Jesus demanding or without compassion, and it doesn't mean His expectations are too high. Telling and teaching others about Jesus Christ—who He is and what He has done for you—should flow naturally from a life surrendered to the lordship of the One who cleansed you, forgave you, redeemed you, transformed you, and provided for you. He didn't leave us on our own to go and make disciples and teach; He provided the Holy Spirit to teach us and to remind us. "But the Advocate, the Holy Spirit, whom the Father will send in my name, will teach you all things and will remind you of everything I have said to you" (John 14:26). Bonhoeffer says, "Obedience to the call of Jesus never lies within our own power."[17]

In what ways is the Holy Spirit teaching you and encouraging you to become a disciple of Christ?

In what ways is the Holy Spirit teaching you and encouraging you to disciple others?

Scripture of Challenge/Encouragement:

> David also said to Solomon his son, "Be strong and courageous, and do the work. Do not be afraid or discouraged, for the LORD God, my God, is with you. He will not fail you or forsake you until all the work for the service of the temple of the LORD is finished." (1 Chronicles 28:20)

Prayer: Meditate on David's words to Solomon, then pray and ask God to help you apply this instruction to your life in making disciples.

WEEK 8

ఴ

OBEDIENCE

Last week we talked about the Great Commission. Since your last meeting, what insights did God give you about this topic?

This week we will learn why we must understand obedience. Our obedience to Jesus's commands will reveal who we belong to. Are we our own, going our own way (Isaiah 53:6), or have we taken up our cross daily and followed Christ (Luke 9:23)? As we've said, Jesus commanded us to go, make disciples, baptize them, and teach them.

The follower of Christ is one who obeys the command. Look up Romans 1:5–6. Write out these verses.

What do these verses teach you about your faith?

Therefore, what does this teach you about the importance of obedience?

Look up 2 Corinthians 12:9. Write out this verse.

What does this verse teach you about grace?

Look up Ephesians 2:8. Write out this verse.

What does this verse teach you about your salvation?

Faith and obedience are the same scarlet cord, split then twined together. This cord connects heaven and our hearts.

GOD (Heaven)

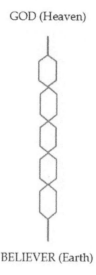

BELIEVER (Earth)

Bonhoeffer explains the relationship between faith and obedience as follows:

> The road to faith passes through obedience to the call of Jesus. Unless a definite step is demanded, the call vanishes into thin air, and if men imagine that they can follow Jesus without taking this step, they are deluding themselves . . . Two propositions hold good and are equally true: only he who believes is obedient, and only he who is obedient believes . . . For faith is only real when there is obedience, never without it, and faith only becomes faith in the act of obedience.
>
> Since, then, we cannot adequately speak of obedience as the consequence of faith, and since we must never forget the indissoluble unity of the two, we must place the one proposition that only he who believes is obedient alongside the other, that only he who is obedient believes. In the one case faith is the condition of obedience, and in the other obedience the

condition of faith. In exactly the same way in which obedience is called the consequence of faith, it must also be called the presupposition of faith.

Only the obedient believe. If we are to believe, we must obey a concrete command. Without this preliminary step of obedience, our faith will only be pious humbug, and lead us to the grace which is not costly.[18]

How do the following Scriptures support this commentary regarding the connection between faith and obedience? Read James 1:22–24 and 2:14–26.

According to James 2:17, faith without action is _____.

In James 2:22, how was Abraham's faith made complete?

James 2:26 sums it up with a telling analogy. "As the body without the spirit is _____, so faith without deeds is _____."

Our obedience to the teachings of Jesus Christ is the measuring stick of our faith. Obedience is action—actively doing what we are instructed to do. Merely talking about it is nothing more than lip service. Jesus told His disciples the night before the crucifixion, "This is to my Father's glory, that you bear much fruit, showing yourselves to be my disciples" (John 15:8). Jesus taught His disciples, and His Word still teaches us to love Him with all our hearts. How do we love Him with all our hearts? John tells us: "And this is love: that we walk in obedience to his commands" (2 John 1:6).

The last command Jesus taught His followers was: "Go and make disciples of all nations, baptizing them in the name of the Father and of the Son and of the Holy Spirit, and teaching them to obey everything I have commanded you" (Matthew 28:19–20).

What exactly does this mean? What does going and making disciples of all nations look like in everyday life? However you answer those questions, most of us have neglected this teaching. We have second-guessed, rearranged, modified, dumbed down, passed off, and even ignored this Commission. The church has relegated this command to the pastor and/or evangelism committee as well as a special group we put on a pedestal (missionaries). We give to the missions fund to absolve ourselves. Is it unbiblical for an established body of believers to send others to spread the gospel and establish new churches? No, not at all. We will look into the book of Acts for more on this in a minute. However, here in America, we neglect the Great Commission not because of a lack of finances or abilities, but because of our own attitudes and selfishness. It's easier to give a special group the task of going and making disciples than it is to accept that the Great Commission is a command to all believers.

David Platt offers an uncompromising take on this subject. He says,

> I wonder if we have in some ways intentionally and in other ways unknowingly erected lines of defense against the global purpose God has for our lives. It's not uncommon to hear Christians say, "Well, not everyone is called to foreign missions," or more specifically, "I am not called to foreign missions." When we say this, we are usually referring to foreign missions as an optional program in the church for a faithful few who apparently are called to that. In this mindset, missions is a compartmentalized program of the church, and select folks are good at missions and passionate about missions. Meanwhile, the rest of us are willing to watch the missions slide shows when the missionaries come home, but in the end God has just not called most of us to do this missions thing.
>
> But where in the Bible is missions ever identified as an optional program in the church? We have just seen that we were all created by God, saved from our sins, and blessed by God to make his glory known in all the world. Indeed, Jesus himself has not merely called us to go to all nations;

he has created us and commanded us to go to all nations. We have taken his command, though, and reduced it to a calling—something that only a few people receive.

I find it interesting that we don't do this with other words from Jesus. We take Jesus' command in Matthew 28 to make disciples of all nations, and we say, "That means other people." But we look at Jesus' command in Matthew 11:28, "Come to me, all you who are weary and burdened, and I will give you rest," and we say, "Now, that means me." But we take Jesus' promise in Acts 1:8 that the Spirit will lead us to the ends of the earth, and we say, "That means some people." But we take Jesus' promise in John 10:10 that we will have abundant life, and we say, "That means me."

In the process we have unnecessarily (and unbiblically) drawn a line of distinction, assigning the *obligations* of Christianity to a few while keeping the *privileges* of Christianity for us all. In this way we choose to send off other people to carry out the global purpose of Christianity while the rest of us sit back because we're "just not called to that."[19]

This excerpt is thought provoking and, to some, even questionable. His point is that all Christians are called to go into all the world and preach the gospel, and that sending "professional" missionaries doesn't fulfill this command. What do you think? While Scripture doesn't make note of professional missionaries, we do see evidence of a local body sending others off to do mission work by winning converts and establishing churches. Read Acts 13:1–5 for evidence of Saul (Paul) and his companions being sent off to do the work to which God had called them. The rest of the book of Acts records the other journeys of Paul as a missionary of the gospel.

What do you think about Platt's words regarding the church and its negligence of the Great Commission?

Let's look at Matthew 28:19–20 again. How can all believers obey the command to go and make disciples of all nations, regardless of their finances, employment, family, and abilities? The original Greek and its grammatical structure of these verses will help us gain understanding. Simplified, "Go" is translated "as you are going" or "in your going." And "all nations" means "a race, a nation, the nations—as distinct from Israel."[20]

To me, this means that as we go about our lives, we should make disciples of all races of people we contact. For some, that means locally. For others, it means across the state. For still others, it means around the country or to foreign soil. The key to obedience is asking God where He wants you to go and then going there.

Why do you think the church has become weak in this teaching of the Great Commission?

We could list numerous and various reasons, including lack of knowledge of the command, not understanding how to carry it out, fear of rejection, and not knowing what to say. For some, complacency is a problem. They are satisfied with life and church as they are. Others would say they simply don't want to obey this command, and others think they don't have time. Unbelief can be a factor as well. Some people don't believe God's Word, don't believe God can use them. Or perhaps others have tried to make disciples, but other believers have questioned their methods and shot down their nontraditional ideas. Next week we will explore two other reasons people don't obey the Commission: lack of commitment and adherence to tradition.

Scripture of Challenge/Encouragement:

> But you will receive power when the Holy Spirit comes on
> you; and you will be my witnesses in Jerusalem, and in all
> Judea and Samaria, and to the ends of the earth. (Acts 1:8)

Prayer: Meditate on Acts 1:8 and how the verse applies to us today. Then write a prayer thanking God for the people He puts as potential converts and disciples in your path, locally and away from home. Ask Him to help you recognize the opportunities He gives as you go.

WEEK 9

ᐰ

COMMITMENT VS. TRADITION

Last week we talked about obedience. Since your last meeting, what insights did God give you about this topic?

We ended last week's lesson with a serious look at how the church has become weak in teaching discipleship and why. This week we will delve deeper into two of those reasons.

First, laziness and selfishness rear their ugly heads in lack of commitment. Folks these days do not like to commit themselves. People want commitment from others, but all they offer in exchange is connection. Those who are lost need commitment from the church, not just connection.

Jesus offered commitment when He came to earth. John the Baptist preached, "Look, the Lamb of God, who takes away the sin of the world!" (John 1:29). Jesus committed to coming here as the Lamb of

God to suffer God's wrath for the sin of mankind. He also committed to dying in our place. In turn, He called His disciples to commit to following Him. Calling them, Jesus said, "Come, follow me, and I will send you out to fish for people" (Matthew 4:19). These words were a call to commitment. To leave behind life as we know it and start a new life of discipling others, we must become fishers of men.

The local church struggles severely with commitment, which baffles me since our whole relationship with Christ hinges on commitment. Jesus said in John 15:5, "Apart from me you can do nothing." Psalm and Proverbs agree. Psalm 37:5 says, "Commit your way to the LORD; trust in him." And Proverbs 16:3 says, "Commit to the LORD whatever you do, and your plans will succeed." Second Chronicles 16:9 confirms this too. It says, "For the eyes of the LORD range throughout the earth to strengthen those whose hearts are fully committed to him."

Look up 1 Peter 4:19. What does this verse teach you about commitment?

How does that verse relate to the Great Commission?

We see sufficient evidence that the local church and the Church in general suffer greatly from lack of commitment. This age-old problem plagued the Israelites too. God, through His prophets, continually exhorted His people to commitment. Look up the following Scriptures and record the evidence of God exhorting His people to commitment.

Deuteronomy 10:12–13:

Joshua 22:5:

1 Samuel 12:24:

Jeremiah 38:20:

Look up 1 Kings 8:61 and write it out.

Here Solomon uttered a prayer to God when blessing Israel at the temple's dedication. How can this verse encourage us to fulfill the Great Commission?

In order for disciples of Christ to obey the commands in the Great Commission, our hearts must be fully committed to the Lord our God. But we frequently confuse commitment to Him with commitment to the traditions of a denomination. This is a killer to disciple-making, baptizing, and teaching converts to obey all Jesus commanded. Jesus's commands were short and few, wrapped and rooted in love. (See Matthew 22:37–40, John 15:17, Matthew 28:19–20.) It is true, Jesus taught on an array of subjects, and each teaching emphasized serving others by going the extra mile and forgiving always. (See the Sermon on the Mount: Matthew 5, 6, 7.) In fact, Jesus plainly stated, "Come to me, all you who are weary and burdened, and I will give you rest. Take my yoke upon you and learn from me, for I am gentle and humble in heart, and you will find rest for your souls. For my yoke is easy and my burden is light" (Matthew 11:28–30).

Jesus's commands and teachings were not new, but they were fresh and spoken with love and compassion, untangled from the yoke of pharisaical tradition and manmade "laws." Matthew 15:1–3 says, "Then some Pharisees and teachers of the law came to Jesus from Jerusalem and asked, 'Why do your disciples break the tradition of the elders? They don't wash their hands before they eat!' Jesus replied, 'And why do you break the command of God for the sake of your tradition?'"

What traditions do you think have weakened the local church and handicapped it to the point that it makes no disciples? Circle the following examples below and/or write your own.

Unwillingness to change methods

Structure of service

Relying on preacher and/or teachers

Relying on missionaries

Thinking the building is here, so people should come

Service times

Being churchgoers rather than Christ-followers

American culture

The group of people Jesus challenged the most and scolded the harshest were the Pharisees. They were the religious elite, the establishment, the leaders of the local synagogue. Look up the following Scriptures. List the ways in which Jesus scolded the Pharisees.

Matthew 6:2:

Matthew 6:5:

Matthew 6:16:

Matthew 9:10–12:

Matthew 12:1–8:

Matthew 12:22–37:

Matthew 15:1–20:

Matthew 23:1–39:

Traditions in and of themselves are not sinful, nor are traditions bad. In fact, traditions have their own purpose in establishing continuity and providing a sense of home and nostalgia. Traditions are also tools for teaching our children. What traditions in the local church do you find beneficial?

However, traditions become a hindrance when we elevate them to holy status or when they become uncompromising, stifle growth, build barriers, or prevent human needs from being met. Traditions become a problem when people confuse them with biblical doctrine. Traditions become a crisis when the Great Commission goes unfulfilled.

Bill Hull offers some informative commentary on this topic:

> A real challenge in disciplemaking is the extracting of people from the yoke of traditions that hinder their spiritual lives. Men and women who are established in the four basics of foundations of the Christian life (Scripture, prayer, fellowship, and witnessing) will experience a trust in the sovereignty of God. This trust leads to personal security, thus reducing the compulsion to control or limit what God is doing. A secure person enjoys the creative spirit of God and looks forward to the next invasion of the supernatural into the mundane. Jesus did not bow down to counterproductive traditions. He spoke out against them as superfluous stumbling blocks that create more trouble

than they are worth. The modern-day disciplemaker can do the same. We need to be enthusiastic about the *right* things. Since everything we do teaches, the impression we leave will be made more by practicing than by preaching.

People who start with hearts aflame rise quickly to leadership in the local church. After a steady dose of administrative headaches, however, the flame often dies out, the heart grows cold. Churches are sometimes organized to administer in-house maintenance at the expense of helping people grow. The duties of necessary church administration should be shared and rotated so that all leaders have the refreshing opportunity periodically to engage in person-to-person ministry. The gifted administrator should be no less established in Scripture, prayer, fellowship, and witnessing than the gifted teacher. When a disciple deals only with buildings and grounds, he begins to believe that the most important aspect of church life is well-kept facilities or consistent cash flow. Conversely, when a disciple deals only with prayer, Bible study, and witnessing, he begins to consider administrative work boring and unspiritual. The proper placing of spiritual gifts is vital to success in the long haul, but variety of experience and appreciation of others' abilities will make for a well-rounded disciple. Furthermore, if administrative personnel are given a ministry sabbatical periodically, they will keep their spiritual life fresh.

Jesus was constantly being confronted by the religious legalists of his day. Legalism is the measuring of spirituality by external behavior. Mark 2:23–3:6 records a classic confrontation over technical obedience to the Law. Parallel accounts are found in Matthew 12:1–21 and Luke 6:1–11. The plot was now thickening as the Jews conspired to kill Jesus.

Jesus taught men to minister with both feet in the world. The best way to reach the needy is to be with them. Without contact, there can be no impact. The Master encountered, as most of his followers will, opposition in traditional religious quarters. Disciples on the front lines for Jesus sometimes get jabbed in the back. Learning to deal with such criticism for being effective in outreach is vital to survival in the harvest field. This was the very problem Jesus faced.[21]

Read Mark 2:23–3:6, Matthew 12:1–21, and Luke 6:1–11 (the accounts mentioned in the above excerpt).

What law did the Pharisees accuse Jesus and the disciples of breaking?

How did Jesus refute the Pharisees' claims?

What biblical truth was Jesus trying to teach in His response to the Pharisees?

In Mark 3:4–5 we learn what Jesus thought of the Pharisees and their accusations. What can we learn from this?

Give a modern-day example you think is similar to these accounts.

Do you think the local church is guilty of cultural bias or prejudice? If so, do you think these views hinder it from making disciples? Explain.

Do you think the church is known more for what we are against rather than what we are for? Explain.

In *Jesus Christ: Disciplemaker*, the author claims:

> The fatal mistake of the Pharisees is still common today among evangelical Christians. We have mistakenly identified the unbeliever as the enemy rather than the victim of the enemy. We have erected unnecessary barriers between ourselves and the very ones we pray to reach. These barriers are usually cultural, not theological.
>
> We often communicate a legalistic attitude that says, "If you practice certain activities, you are not welcome in the Christian community."
>
> Therefore, the nonbeliever receives an inflexible, judgmental attitude from the very ones who should be accepting him or her. The Christian community must keep the unbeliever's view of salvation uncluttered with cultural bias. We need to keep the message of salvation simple and pure, just as Jesus modeled for us.[22]

Scripture of Challenge/Encouragement:

> And may your hearts be fully committed to the LORD
> our God, to live by his decrees and obey his commands,
> as at this time. (1 Kings 8:61)

Prayer: Meditate on the verse from 1 Kings; it is from King Solomon's prayer of dedication of the temple. Write out a prayer of thanks to God that you are His temple, and ask God for His grace to live in obedience to His commands.

PART 2 SUMMARY

In part 2, "The Commission: Understanding Discipleship," we have examined the Great Commission, its directives, and the core of the Commission—obedience. We also looked at ways we can accomplish this command of Christ without allowing tradition and cultural bias to prevent us from fulfilling the call.

From this part of the Bible study, what insights and/or convictions has the Holy Spirit impressed upon you?

౭౨

THE CHARGE: PRACTICING DISCIPLESHIP (JESUS AND THE TWELVE: THE ORIGINAL SMALL GROUP)

There is now underway a major shift in many churches of the Western world—a shift from clergy-centered ministry to a ministry of laypeople equipped for service. This change in the Western world is gradually taking place all around us. Christian leaders are lovingly but firmly leading the church out of the misconceptions and mistakes of the past to the proper scriptural pattern intended by God. The goal of many individual churches is to transform a congregation of spectators being led by a minister into an army of ministers being led by a pastor.[23]

Finish without fizzling. Never stop trusting, serving, following Jesus Christ.[24]

This part of the study, The Charge: Practicing Discipleship, focuses on Jesus and His first twelve disciples—the model He presented to spread the good news to whosoever would come. This part of the study is an examination of Jesus's model. Who He is, what He did, and how He did it—that's our standard. As followers of Jesus Christ, we should be award-winning historians of Jesus and His life, don't you think? How will we know what to do if we don't first know what He did and how He did it?

Practicing Discipleship breaks down Jesus's earthly ministry into five parts: Come and See; Come, Follow Me; Go, Be Like Me; Go a New Way; and Remain in Me. Jesus established the plan of making disciples and modeled that plan in the three years of His ministry. Making disciples was never meant to be a program or a series of mundane classes taught with a lesson book. It was never meant to be complicated or labor intensive. Making disciples should occur naturally as we form relationships with people, just as Jesus did with the Twelve. As we encounter people, make acquaintances, and form friendships, we are to let people know who we are and whose we are. This means we should share Christ—let them know who He is and what He has done for us. Jesus's method of making disciples was a natural, gradual, intentional process. Don't miss that last word: process. Disciple-making is a process. It will happen in stages, and it will take time. Let's examine each phase of this process.

WEEK 10

℘

COME AND SEE: ENCOUNTERING CHRIST

Last week we talked about commitment vs. tradition. Since your last meeting, what insights did God give you about this topic?

This first period of discipleship is the initial person-to-person encounter Jesus had with John, Andrew, Peter, Philip, and Nathanael. The Gospel of John is the only one of the four gospels to record this first brief period of discipleship. The books of Matthew, Mark, and Luke are known as the Synoptic Gospels because they give a synopsis of Jesus's earthly ministry from a relatively similar perspective. John's gospel deviated from their perspective in that John's sole purpose was to settle the fact that Jesus is almighty God. Nonetheless, John provided some informative details of the first disciples. John 1:35 states, "The next day John [the Baptist] was there again with two of his disciples." The "next day" is the day after John the Baptist baptized Jesus (John 1:32–34). John the Baptist had been preaching, witnessing to *his disciples* of the coming Messiah: "Look, the Lamb of God, who takes away the sin of the world!" (John 1:29). The Bible is clear that Andrew was one of the two of John's disciples (John 1:40). I think it stands to reason John (the writer of this gospel) is the other, since he was the only one to record this in his gospel. However, that's opinion, not biblical fact.

Read John 1:35–42. Summarize what occurs in this passage.

How did Jesus address John's two disciples who followed Him? Why do you think He addressed them with that question?

What can we learn from this initial encounter of Jesus and His two would-be disciples?

Hull writes:

> A vital principle of discipleship emerges at this point: Do not recruit people for anything without first allowing them to have their curiosity assuaged. Jesus was not afraid to reveal the small print in the contract. We get the distinct impression from the passage that Jesus desired to

make it easy to say no. He did not employ the misguided habit of twenty-first century Christendom of "quick-pitching" people into commitments. When this hasty method is utilized, the recruit normally takes off like a rocket, only to fall back later to the earth like a rock. After such a misfire, restoration is nearly impossible, a very messy business. We must not be intimidating when we invite others to take a look at the Master. Indeed, at the outset, Jesus himself launched his plan to rescue planet Earth with the simple invitation to come and see.[25]

In John 1:35–42, why do you think it's significant that two of John's disciples are the first two Jesus called?

Exactly what invitation did Jesus extend in verse 39?

How do Psalm 34:8 and 1 Peter 2:3 support Jesus's invitation to these two?

What do you think Jesus means by "Come and see"? What are some modern, practical examples of this "Come and see" phase of discipling others?

Again, Hull says:

> John was serving in a ministry of preparation, provoking an interest in the Messiah to come. When Jesus, the true Messiah, arrived on the scene, John's season of preparation was over. He had successfully set the stage for the great event of salvation, but it was time for him to gracefully step aside.
>
> Part of the discipling process is this phase of preparation, sustaining the believers while the seeds of commitment are germinating. We need to recognize the value of the work accomplished by someone like John the Baptist. He was an advance man, a forerunner who prepared the way. Such a ministry is a natural prelude to commitment. In our churches today, we need to monitor and nurture the spiritual fledglings, as John did so well.
>
> Typical ministries of preparation such as Sunday schools, music programs, and fellowship groups provide a forum in which the observant builder of disciples can watch and wait until a person is ripe and ready. Such programs are not to be discounted as non-disciple-making ministries, but it must be recognized that they do not usually provide training in ministry skills. These "holding tank" ministries are vital to successful discipling, for without them we would not have a primary opportunity to gather in those who are not presently prepared for more serious involvement. We must be patient—waiting and watching for the proper moment—for the Spirit of God prepares the hearts of disciples for a certain moment when they stand up and say, "Here I am, Lord, reporting for duty." This was the case when the two men left John at the appointed moment to follow the Messiah.[26]

In John 1:41, what can we learn from Andrew and apply to our lives?

What is the first thing Jesus said to Simon?

Do you think Jesus knew what kind of man Simon was when He called him? Why or why not?

How does this verse show us who Jesus calls and how we should disciple others?

According to *Jesus Christ: Disciplemaker*:

> As Peter stood there before Christ for the very first time, the Master demonstrated another key principle of discipleship. He said to the uncultivated fisherman, "You will be called Cephas," which means "rock" (John 1:42). When Jesus looked into the eyes of Peter, he saw more than meets the mere human eye. He knew that this was an impulsive, presumptuous, take-charge type, who would promise the moon and try anything at least once. Yet Jesus also saw a strong heart and a rare brand of courage. A man such as Peter, when filled with God's Spirit, becomes a rock of stability. Jesus saw a man who

would stand strong several years later on the day of Pentecost, preaching the word boldly.

Jesus saw in Peter what he sees in each of us—nothing that a miracle cannot cure. Jesus sees his followers for what they will be, not for what they are in "the spiritual raw." Everyone is a candidate for something, and there are no exceptions. Regardless of what we might see in a person, pro or con, there is much more than meets the eye, things that only God understands. Here is a primary lesson for those seeking to recruit and develop disciples: *Do not depend on your own conventional wisdom. Seek the guidance of the Holy Spirit for spiritual understanding.*[27]

Read John 1:43–51. Summarize what occurs in this passage.

Jesus's invitation to Philip is direct. What is it? (v. 43)

How is "Come and see" different from "Come and follow Me"?

Read John 2:1–11. On the third day of the "Come and see" period, Jesus took His disciples (Andrew, Peter, Philip, and Nathanael) with Him to a wedding in Cana.

What miracle does Jesus perform at the wedding banquet?

What is significant about the miracle? (v. 11)

Jesus discreetly performed the miracle at the wedding at the persistent request of His mother. However, He did it not so much for her or the wedded couple, but rather as a sign for the disciples as they watched Him closely. Jesus did not publicly perform this miracle of changing water to wine. Both what He did and how He did it teach us a lesson on discipleship. First, it confirms that discipleship is a process. Read verse 4 again.

How did Jesus respond to His mother?

Jesus made this statement several times throughout His earthly ministry. Why do you think He said this instead of revealing Himself to the public all at once? Does this statement help confirm the idea that discipleship is a process?

Moreover, Jesus granted His mother's request, meeting what some may consider an insignificant need—the banquet ran out of beverages. What can we learn from Jesus's willingness to meet needs? Which should concern us more: programs or people? Explain your answer.

Christian leaders should have ministry antennae fully extended, utilizing ordinary situations to allow God to intervene supernaturally, for then people will yearn for more of the same, and they will grow in their commitment. Disciples should eventually come to a point of being prepared to deny themselves anything to be involved in the most exciting enterprise known to the human spirit.

Unfortunately, many move at a breakneck pace. We live in the "fast lane," daily rushing by needs. As one caustic critic has said, "Jesus turned the water into wine, whereas the church has turned the wine into water." The glory of Christ has been seriously diluted in our experience, and thus the life we portray to the world is spiritually unattractive.

These disciples with their well-cultivated hearts now had seeds of the supernatural germinating in their souls, and like so many others who have come after them, they would never be able stop the seeds, their burgeoning faith, from growing. Like blades of grass pushing their way through cracks in the sidewalk, the seeds of thought were maturing, steadily changing the lives of these men. As disciples who are commissioned to train others, we should perpetually expose people to the supernatural, stretching the faith of both them and us. We need to reach out to accept the daily challenges that place us in positions to nurture and motivate others.[28]

In this early phase of discipleship, Jesus not only revealed His glory in working the miracle at Cana, but He also established His authority. Read John 2:12–23.

When Jesus went to the temple during Passover, what did He find occurring in the temple courts?

How did He handle the situation?

Based on the wording and punctuation of the Scriptures, describe Jesus's tone and emotions.

As the Jews questioned Jesus's authority, the disciples observed the scene unfolding before their eyes, but they didn't really get it. They wouldn't understand the full scope of these events until after the resurrection. Yet the disciples observed. They came, and they saw who He was, one step at a time. They watched Jesus not only challenge but also dismantle and disprove the established power and privilege of the religious elite, the Pharisees. Most all of these teachers of the Law were unimpressed and disinterested; they completely rejected who Jesus was. However, one of the men from the ranks of the establishment sought out Jesus, genuinely interested in knowing who He was. That man was Nicodemus. Read John 3:1–15. Also read John 7:45–52 and 19:38–40.

Jesus addressed Nicodemus differently than the disciples. Why do you think He did that?

Did Jesus beg Nicodemus or run after him? How did Jesus witness to Nicodemus?

Did Nicodemus ever become a follower of Christ? Do you see a process whereby he developed faith? (Use the passages above to help you in your answer.)

In this initial "come and see" phase of discipleship, the disciples observed Jesus in several roles in different settings. They had heard John the Baptist teach and proclaim Jesus as the Messiah, the Lamb of God who takes away the sin of the world. They knew of Jesus's humility and submission in baptism and saw Him as the dutiful son granting His mother's request. They recognized His compassion for the wedding guests in the miracle at Cana and watched Him establish His authority as He cleared the temple of the money-changers. And they heard Him stump the religious elite with His explanation of what it means to be born again. Jesus wanted the disciples to taste and see that the Lord is good (Psalm 34:8), hoping they would crave pure spiritual milk and thus grow up in their salvation (1 Peter 2:2).

How many people are "coming and seeing" Jesus in you regularly? What do your thoughts, actions, reactions, and words reveal to others about Christ?

Scripture of Challenge/Encouragement:

> The Spirit and the bride say, "Come!" And let the one who hears say, "Come!" Let the one who is thirsty come; and let the one who wishes take the free gift of the water of life. (Revelation 22:17)

Prayer: Meditate on the verse from Revelation, then thank God for His free gift of salvation, which quenches the deepest thirst of our souls.

WEEK 11

ॐ

COME, FOLLOW ME: ABANDONING ALL FOR THE GOSPEL

Last week we talked about spreading the good news. Since your last meeting, what insights did God give you about this topic?

The call of "Come, follow Me," the second phase of discipleship, is the call to abandon oneself and the attachments and lure of the things of this world. James strongly warned in his letter, "You adulterous people, don't you know that friendship with the world means enmity against God?" (James 4:4). "Come, follow Me" is the call to abandon all for the sake of the gospel. Answering the call of "Come, follow Me" is an intentional, life-altering decision of commitment. Remember Luke 9:23, "Whoever wants to be my disciple must deny themselves and take up their cross daily and follow me." Jesus's call of "Come, follow Me" is radical. Answering the call will change your life. Read Matthew 4:18–22 and Mark 1:14–20.

Summarize the event that occurs in these passages.

Compare the aforementioned Matthew and Mark passages with Luke 5:1–11. (The Gospel of John does not record this event.) The Luke passage gives greater details of the day when Jesus called these four men to be His disciples. The Lake of Gennesaret is another name for the Sea of Galilee. Answer the following questions to see the additional information Luke's account provides that Matthew and Mark's accounts do not.

Was a crowd of people gathered there?

Did Jesus teach the crowd?

Does the passage tell us specifically what Jesus taught?

Where did Jesus teach?

What miracle did Jesus perform?

What do you think was the purpose of the miracle?

What effect did the miracle have on Peter?

Is this the first encounter between Jesus and Peter, Andrew, James, and John?

How do you know?

What does this teach you about the calling of the disciples and discipleship in general?

Read Luke 5:27–32 and briefly summarize the event documented there.

Describe the type of men Jesus has called to be His disciples so far.

Does this surprise you? Is this what you would expect? Explain.

We may or may not expect Jesus to call these kinds of men, but it should not at all surprise us. Think about the Old Testament heroes of the faith. Father Abraham was an adulterer—technically he was a polygamist (Genesis 16:3–4); Jacob was a thief (Genesis 27:35); Moses was reluctant and a stutterer (Exodus 4:10); Rahab was a prostitute (Joshua 2:1); Naomi was bitter (Ruth 1:20); David was a liar, adulterer, and murderer (2 Samuel 12:7–9); and Jonah was a coward (Jonah 1:3).

These Old Testament saints weren't exactly beacons of virtue. However, who they were and what they did are less important than who they became because of the Spirit of the Lord. And that's the point. The disciples were no different, and neither are you. This motley crew of sinners included uneducated fishermen, a crooked tax collector, a loud-mouthed denier, a zealot, a doubter, a traitor, and a few others thrown in the mix.

Bill Hull offered his thoughts on the choice of disciples when he wrote,

> I find even more astonishing Jesus's choice of personnel to reach the world—not men of means, some elite strata of society, or men of the ecclesiastical establishment, but simple Galilean fishermen, rough and somewhat pedestrian in their thinking, influenced by Jewish passions and prejudices. They were slow to learn and slower still to unlearn. Why would such practical, hardworking, down-to-earth men want to risk it all to pursue an unknown quest?[29]

Why would they? And why would we? This is a question you must ponder and answer. Only afterward will you know why you can effectively disciple another. Ponder and answer. See 1 Corinthians 1:26–29 for further insight.

Write out Jesus's call to the disciples. (Luke 5:27)

Were the disciples given a position in the church, a title, or even a responsibility right away?

Why do you think that was the case?

Hull reasons:

> A principle repeated often in the life of Jesus is *Give people time to make solid decisions.* Jesus didn't rush his men. Consequently, like ripe fruit ready for picking, when the time came, they offered no resistance. Another reason why these men immediately followed Christ is that *they were given an invitation not a responsibility.* "Follow me" is a simple invitation. What is even more impressive than what Jesus said is what he didn't say. He didn't say, "Follow me and I will make you leaders and preachers." Nor did he say, "Peter, the future of the church rests in your hands; you will give the inaugural message for the church." Nor did he say, "John, you will be imprisoned and persecuted

greatly for my sake." He didn't give them enticing promises or specific prophecies because he knew in his wisdom that these men were not prepared to hear them. Jesus understood the hearts of men (John 2:24), and so he knew the disciples' tolerance level for new information. Therefore, even as late as the eve of his crucifixion (16:12), Jesus withheld certain information from them because he knew what they were unable to endure or understand.[30]

Give some practical examples of giving people time to make decisions.

People need to discover, learn, and experience some information and details on their own. Solomon conveyed such wisdom when he penned, "There is a time for everything" (Ecclesiastes 3:1). We should expect change, expect life to be a process and a journey, and expect to learn and know certain truths in their proper time. Just as Hull said, Jesus taught His disciples in stages. He knew how to reveal truth in a way they could process, experience, and then implement.

Throughout Jesus's earthly ministry, news spread about Him (Luke 5:15, Luke 4:14). The religious elite from all around the area came to hear and test Him (Luke 5:17, Matthew 16:1). Crowds continuously gathered around Him, seeking healing (Matthew 8:1, 9:35–36, and 13:2). But He extended His simple yet costly invitation to whosoever. Again, Jesus made it easy for "whosoever" to walk away. He never begged, tricked, or sold the good news with gimmicks like a traveling salesman. Accepting Jesus's invitation was not the same for everyone, as we will see in several passages of Scripture. But the meaning was the same. "Follow Me" is the invitation of abandon. Read Luke 9:57–62 and Mark 10:17–31 for examples. In these two passages, He gives four men (three in Luke and one in Mark) the invitation: Follow Me.

How did each of the four respond? What was each asked to abandon? How did Jesus react to their responses?

Luke 9:57–62

First man:

Second man:

Third man:

Mark 10:17–31

Fourth man:

Other prospective followers had similar encounters with Jesus and the apostles but with different results. The invitation was the same: "Follow Me." It is an invitation of abandon. Read each passage below and note who these people were and how they responded to the invitation.

Luke 19:1–9:

John 4:1–42

Acts 2:42–47:

Acts 10:1–48:

Acts 16:11–15:

How can we apply these Scriptures—Jesus's and the apostles' examples of witnessing—to our lives in discipling others? Include the Luke 9 and Mark 10 passages. Give practical examples of what this might look like in your life.

Think about Jesus and the Twelve. When Jesus began to call His disciples (Peter, Andrew, James, John, and Levi, also known as Matthew), He invited them into His life to share and to teach them in everyday practical living. Jesus set before the Twelve the example; He modeled loving and serving God so they would eventually model living as followers of Christ. The disciples watched Him go and pray alone. They heard Him pray before others. They witnessed His compassion for the crowds as He met their physical needs and then their spiritual needs. They observed Him healing various diseases and deformities and watched Him take on and stump the religious leaders of the day.

Jesus assumed full responsibility: "Follow me and *I* will make you . . ." He would bear the weight of their training. He would not ask of them anything that he himself had not shown them.[31]

Jesus invited the disciples into His life to see how He lived and to watch what He did.

What practical ways can you and I disciple others? Look up 1 Corinthians 11:1 and use it to support your answer.

See also 1 Timothy 4:12, Titus 2:7–8, and Matthew 5:16. How do these verses support 1 Corinthians 11:1?

We, as Christ-followers, are instructed to set a godly example; our daily lives should be a testimony of who Jesus is. The apostle Paul said, "Follow my example, as I follow the example of Christ" (1 Corinthians 11:1). Does the example you set lead others to follow Christ? Please explain.

There are practical and specific ways to disciple others. In the following excerpt, David Platt explains them well.

Think about it. What would be the most effective way for this new follower of Christ to learn to pray? To sign her up for a one-hour-a-week class on prayer? Or invite her personally into your quiet time with God to teach her how to pray?

Similarly, what would be the most effective way for this new follower of Christ to learn to study the Bible? To register her in the next available course on Bible study? Or to sit down with her and walk her through the steps of how you have learned to study the Bible?

This raises the bar in our own Christianity. In order to teach someone else how to pray, we need to know how to pray. In order to help someone else learn how to study the Bible, we need to be active in studying the Bible. But this is the beauty of making disciples. When we take responsibility for helping others grow in Christ, it automatically takes our own relationship with Christ to a new level.[32]

Platt's aforementioned excerpt is powerful and challenging. What about it do you find most challenging?

Platt's statements are at the heart of what it means to disciple others, to invest our lives in the lives of others. Yes, it is time consuming. Yes, it requires effort. Yes, it holds us accountable. Yes, it can be difficult and put us in uncomfortable situations. Yet, it is worth it.

We must remember that today's struggles, hardships, and pain are worth tomorrow's peace, victories, and rewards. We must maintain an eternal perspective rather than a temporal one, as Paul said to the Corinthians: "So we fix our eyes not on what is seen, but on what is unseen, since what is seen is temporary, but what is unseen is eternal" (2 Corinthians 4:18).

Scripture of Challenge/Encouragement:

> And he said to them, "Follow me, and I will make you fishers of men." Immediately they left their nets and followed him. (Matthew 4:19–20 ESV)

Prayer: Meditate on the verse from Matthew, then write out a prayer asking God to help you become a fisher of men (of people).

ಐ

GO, BE LIKE ME

Last week we talked about abandoning all for the gospel. Since your last meeting, what insights did God give you about this topic?

After the disciples had been with Jesus for many months, observing and learning, the time had come for their own assignment. Now Jesus asked them to go and share what He had taught them while they were still under His tutelage. Now they would come out from under the comfortable wing of Christ and into the cold, cruel world of their fellow Jews.

John records that Jesus had taught them what they needed to know: "Then Jesus went up on a mountainside and sat down with his disciples" (John 6:3). They were His, and He had taken on the responsibility to teach them. He had also taught them indirectly as He spoke to the crowds or the Pharisees, and the disciples had seen Him healing the sick (John 6:2), driving out demons (Matthew 12:22), making mute tongues speak (Matthew 9:32–33), causing deaf ears to hear (Mark 7:35), and strengthening lame legs to walk (John 5:7–9).

Now the time came for the disciples' first test. "Jesus called his twelve disciples to him and gave them authority to drive out impure spirits and to heal every disease and sickness" (Matthew 10:1). Jesus had prepared them, explained the harvest to come. Read Matthew 9:37–38 and John 4:34–37.

What did Jesus teach about the harvest?

The time had come for Him to give the disciples their first mission. Jesus called them unto Him to give them the needed guidelines for their assignment. Who did Jesus task with this first assignment to go and reap the harvest? Matthew, Mark, and Luke record the list of disciples whom Jesus deemed apostles and equipped to carry out the mission. John's gospel doesn't record any such list. The following chart is of Matthew 10:2–4, Mark 3:16–19, and Luke 6:14–16.

Matthew	Mark	Luke
Simon	Simon	Simon
Andrew	Andrew	Andrew
James	James	James
John	John	John
Philip	Philip	Philip
Bartholomew	Bartholomew	Bartholomew
Thomas	Thomas	Thomas
Matthew	Matthew	Matthew
James, son of Alphaeus	James, son of Alphaeus	James, son of Alphaeus
Thaddaeus	Thaddaeus	Judas, son of James
Simon the Zealot	Simon the Zealot	Simon the Zealot
Judas Iscariot	Judas Iscariot	Judas Iscariot

Once Jesus designated the disciples as apostles, He proceeded with instructions for this commission. Read Matthew 10:5–42 and then compare the Matthew passage with Mark 6:7–13 and Luke 9:1–6. Matthew's account provided details of the instructions. Notice the instructions came with the authority to do the assigned task. He "gave them authority to drive out evil spirits and to heal every disease and sickness."

What were the instructions? As you read Matthew's account, fill in the following blanks.

Do not go to the _____

Go to the _____

Preach this message _____

Heal the _____

Raise the _____

Cleanse those _____

Drive out _____

Freely you have received; freely _____

Do not take along _____

Stay at _____

Give it your _____

If the home is deserving, _____

If anyone will not welcome you, _____

Be on your _____

Do not worry about _____

You will be given _____

It will not be you, but _____

When you are persecuted in one place, _____

Do not be afraid of those who _____

Whoever acknowledges me before men_____

But whoever disowns me before men_____

Jesus continued to elaborate on His instructions before sending the Twelve out on their own for the first time. In verses 34–36 He warned, "Do not suppose that I have come to bring peace to the earth. I did not come to bring peace, but a sword. For I have come to turn 'a man against his father, a daughter against her mother, a daughter-in-law against her mother-in-law—a man's enemies will be the members of his own household.'"

What truth is Jesus teaching them (us)?

How do you reconcile those verses (Matthew 10:34–36) with John 14:27 and 16:33?

The Twelve returned to Jesus and reported to Him all that had happened on their first solo mission. "The apostles gathered around Jesus and reported to him all they had done and taught" (Mark 6:30). Jesus wanted them to decompress and debrief with Him in private. Mark recorded, "Then, because so many people were coming and going that they did not even have a chance to eat, he said to them, 'Come with me by yourselves to a quiet place and get some rest'" (Mark 6:31).

Discipleship can be tiring, it is time-consuming, and it requires compassion. Without compassion for the many lost people wandering in darkness and held captive by their sin, discipleship (ministry) becomes a burden. Jesus knew the disciples needed some time alone to rest, yet when the crowds followed them, He showed compassion (Mark 6:34). Jesus said they were "like sheep without a shepherd" (v. 34). Instead of dismissing the five thousand people, Jesus used the opportunity to teach the disciples further. This was when Jesus performed the miracle of feeding the five thousand. Read Mark 6:35–44 and Luke 9:10–17.

Was the miracle an activity or ministry? What's the difference?

What does this passage teach you about time management and the needs of people in the process of discipleship? Give a personal example of a situation you feel is similar and what you learned from that experience.

> The difference between ministry and activity is concern. Mere activity wears us out; ministry builds us up. When warmth is felt, the message is heard. *Compassion is the motivational basis of meaningful ministry.* The difficulty of ministry, the carnality of Christians, and the corruption of human nature will smash any good vision. Therefore, when pressed to the wall it is vitally important for the disciples to *care* enough to keep on going.
>
> The disciples could have explained the ministry of Jesus in one word—compassion. If you truly care about people, they will beat a path to your door. I am not saying that you will become famous and need bodyguards or secret travel plans. But meeting needs never goes out of style. The foundation of ministry is caring, and the vital link to a caring spirit is a close communion with our heavenly Father.[33]

There is another biblical account of disciples being sent out during Jesus's earthly ministry. Luke's gospel is the only recording of Jesus sending out the Seventy-two. Read Luke 10:1–23. Note the similarities between Jesus's instructions to the Twelve and then to the Seventy-two.

What do you think Jesus taught by sending them out two by two?

How does verse 2 speak to you? Is the "work" Jesus referred to the use of one's spiritual gift or discipleship? What's the difference?

The purpose of spiritual gifts is to edify the body of Christ in a local assembly or as a whole. Discipleship is investing our life in Christ in the lives of others. The distinction is necessary, as church culture has adopted the Pareto principle: 20 percent of the people doing 80 percent of the work. The other 80 percent of church members sit in a pew. Also, in many cases, the local church has been reduced to a building serving its members. However, true discipleship occurs outside the meeting times of the local assembly. The point is this: you do not have to have the gift of teaching or preaching to disciple someone. Every believer is commanded to go and make disciples (Matthew 28:19).

In Luke, chapter 10, list the applicable truths of discipleship Jesus taught in:

verse 3:

verse 4:

verses 5–6:

verse 7:

verse 8:

verse 9:

verses 10–11:

Did Jesus go behind the ones He sent out? What does this teach us regarding discipling others?

Discipleship, and ministry in general, are meant to be done with others, in a relationship. Luke writes that Jesus "sent them two by two" (10:1). The kingdom of God is a family of believers who make up the whole body of Christ. Each has their own specific gift, and those spiritual gifts work together like individual piano keys, played together to create harmony (Romans 12:16). So it is with disciples of Christ. And we are called to live and function as a body in unity. Read Ephesians 4:11–16.

Why did Jesus give us different spiritual gifts?

We work best when we work together. Kingdom work was never meant to be a solo task. Even Jesus worked in tandem with the Father. Read John 14:10–12. What do these verses teach us about Jesus's relationship with the Father?

Jesus did not send out the Seventy-two on their own as He had the Twelve; He followed behind them. Luke 10:1 goes on to say He "sent them two by two ahead of him to every town and place where he was about to go." This larger group may have been made up of those who had become followers, who had heard Him teach and even witnessed many miracles of healing. Nonetheless, this group had not been with Him as the disciples had during their more intensive training. It stands to reason, then, that He was coming not far behind. Jesus whetted their appetites for witnessing, discipleship, and ministry, but He did it in a way for them to be successful. He set them up to win by coming behind them.

What are some practical examples of opportunities less spiritually mature believers might be directed toward in order to gain experience?

In your assessment of the local church, are less spiritually mature believers often given tasks to set them up to win or set them up to fail? In other words, do we often encourage or ask people to fill a role before they are ready? Please explain.

The local church leadership structure should be one in which mature believers partner with new believers and/or less spiritually mature believers rather than merely assigning tasks or positions. Partnering fosters relationships and promotes discipleship within the congregation, which strengthens the core of the church.

Scripture of Challenge/Encouragement:

> As you go, proclaim this message: "The kingdom of
> heaven has come near." (Matthew 10:7)

Prayer: Meditate on this verse from Matthew, then write out a prayer
thanking God for the opportunities to proclaim His message and ask
Him for the grace to boldly proclaim it.

WEEK 13

&

GO A NEW WAY

Last week we talked about ministering like Jesus. Since your last meeting, what insights did God give you about this topic?

During the "Go a New Way" period of the disciples' training, Jesus moved His ministry from the synagogue to the streets and shifted His method of teaching from sermons to parables. He began to focus on those eager to hear the good news rather than the close-minded religious elite who had rejected who He was.

What is a parable? Why did Jesus choose this method to teach the Twelve? Did this become Jesus's exclusive method to convey biblical truths? Did Jesus intend to confuse them, or us, for that matter? A parable is generally a short story centered around common cultural and/or earthly practices to convey a universal biblical truth. Jesus shifted to teaching through parables for several reasons: to convey universal truth, to keep from revealing Himself completely because His mission was not yet accomplished, to conceal truth from the Pharisees, and to proclaim prophecy. Jesus used historical context, culture, and situations of everyday life to teach through analogy, comparison, and contrast.

The parable of the sower is one of the first parables Jesus taught. Matthew, Mark, and Luke all record this parable, and all these gospel writers place this parable in conjunction with Jesus sending out the disciples for the first time. The parable of the sower served to teach the disciples about witnessing and discipling others as they went "out like sheep among wolves." He went on to instruct them, saying, "Be as shrewd as snakes and as innocent as doves" (Matthew 10:16).

Read the parable of the sower in Matthew 13:1–23.

Did the disciples understand the parable at first?

What was Christ's answer for teaching through parables?

What do you think this parable is teaching? What was its purpose, then and now?

Read Matthew 13:24–30 and 36–43, the parable of the weeds.

Again, did the disciples ask to have the parable explained?

What does this teach you about your own discipleship and your discipling of others?

What truth was conveyed in this parable?

Read the parable of the hidden treasure and the parable of the pearl in Matthew 13:44–46.

How do these parables support what we have been studying about "Come and See" and "Come, Follow Me"?

Two other prominent events occur in this "Go a New Way" period. Jesus had been slowly revealing Himself to His disciples and teaching them important truths along the way. These truths stumped the high and mighty, showy Pharisees. They also broke down cultural barriers for gentiles (John 4:43–51 and Mark 7:24–30), those of mixed race (Luke 10:29–37), women (John 4:7–29), and lepers (Mark 1:40–45). Jesus took the way it had always been, wadded it up, and threw it out. He dared to challenge and change the status quo.

Yes, Jesus's life, death, burial, and resurrection said there is a new way, a better way. He took the good and made it great, the ordinary and made it extraordinary. Jesus truly modeled what it means to love as God has loved us (John 15:12) and to serve as a follower of Christ (John 12:26) by elevating the servant on earth to the highest social status in heaven (Matthew 23:11). Yet the Gospel of Luke recorded a few verses as a gentle reminder of a foundational truth for the follower: worship of the Master is paramount. It comes before serving others.

The scene unfolds in the small village of Bethany on the outskirts of Jerusalem in the home of Lazarus and his two sisters, Mary and Martha. The disciples were with Jesus, of course, observing this seemingly uneventful visit. However, as He usually did, Jesus capitalized on the moment to teach an important lesson: balance.

Read Luke 10:38–42. What was Martha busy doing?

What about Mary?

How did Jesus respond to Martha's complaining?

What does this teach us about balance in ministry?

Martha was busy serving and making all the preparations for the visit of Jesus and the disciples. Those preparations must have been time-consuming, hard work. She was making the house ready and cooking for thirteen extra men! She had no Mini Maid or caterer on speed dial. There was a lot of work to be done, and she was the one doing it.

All the while, Mary sat at the Lord's feet. She hung on His every word like the last oak leaf in the fall. She was quiet, she was still, and she was unaware of Martha's need for help.

Or was she? Maybe Martha was a natural-born complainer, and Mary had learned to tune her out over the years. Or maybe Mary just needed to spend time feasting at the feet of the Lord. Mary and Martha present a real dichotomy we all face: hard work vs. rest, both physical and spiritual. Both elements of the Christian life are necessary if we want to live in obedience. A faith that won't fizzle is one that is rekindled, and if we've learned anything thus far in this study, it's that we weren't called to fizzle or quit. We were called to follow Christ. We were called to go and make disciples. In our going and making, baptizing and teaching, we must not neglect worship of Jesus or feasting on the written Word. Just as physical health requires a balanced, nutritious diet, so spiritual health requires balance in doing *for* the Savior and listening *to* the Savior.

The other prominent event to occur during this period of the disciples' training is known as the transfiguration. Jesus had sent out the disciples on their own to minister. When they reported back to Him, they quickly discovered that the teaching was not over. Jesus had more to teach, more to model, and more for the disciples to learn. Throughout His earthly ministry, Jesus told several different people that His time had not come or the time to reveal Himself had not come. Look up the following verses and record with whom Jesus is speaking, what He is speaking about, and why.

John 2:4:

John 7:6:

John 7:30:

John 8:20:

Jesus also instructed several different people not to tell anyone who He was. Such verses read in isolation and not studied in their proper context can lead to confusion. Look up the following verses and record what Jesus said and to whom.

Mark 1:40–45:

Mark 3:11–12:

Mark 5:37–43:

Mark 8:22–26:

Jesus also warned several of those who had received healing not to tell anyone. Jesus's actions are explained in the following verses. Look up each of these and record how these verses explain what He meant when He said His time had not yet come.

Matthew 26:18:

Mark 14:35:

John 13:1:

John 17:1:

How do Ecclesiastes 3:1–8 and Acts 1:7 support the previous verses we have read on this topic?

What do these verses teach us, not only about our heavenly Father and His plans and purposes for Jesus's earthly ministry, but for our own ministry of being a disciple and making disciples?

At the transfiguration, the time had come for Christ to reveal Himself in all of His glory to His inner circle: Peter, James, and John. Luke recorded this moment, giving a time reference: "About eight days after Jesus said this . . ." (Luke 9:28). Read Luke 9:28–36 and then answer the following questions.

Where did this event take place?

Who was there?

What did Peter want to do?

How did God the Father appear, and what did He say?

Why do you think Jesus gave privilege to Peter, James, and John for this experience? What can we learn from this?

Why just them, and why would they keep this to themselves? For now, or for always? (See Mark 9:9.)

How does God's appearance in an enveloping cloud correlate with God speaking to some of the Old Testament saints? See Exodus 13:21–22, Leviticus 16:2, Numbers 16:42, 1 Kings 8:10–12.

Obviously it was important for the inner circle to understand that Jesus was God. Jesus transfigured before them, standing alongside Moses and Elijah in their glorified bodies. The sight of the three heavenly, eternal bodies would prove that Jesus was God and would confirm the supremacy and preeminence of Jesus Christ (Colossians 1:15–20). This is key; it is paramount to our own faith. Jesus is God. Jesus being God changes the trajectory of religion. For the Christian, it is no longer religion, but rather it is a relationship between the sinner and the Creator. We can have this relationship only because the Creator clothed Himself in flesh (Colossians 2:9) and came down to His creation to reconcile His greatest creation unto Himself. That reconciliation was made possible only because God in the flesh shed His own sinless blood (Acts 20:28) to cleanse us from the sin that had corrupted us. Jesus is God. He said, "Anyone who has seen me has seen the Father" (John 14:9).

John's gospel records the following eight "I Am" statements.

"Then Jesus declared, '_____. He who comes to me will never go hungry, and he who believes in me will never be thirsty'" (John 6:35).

"When Jesus spoke again to the people, he said, '_____ _____. Whoever follows me will never walk in darkness, but will have the light of life'" (John 8:12).

"Very truly I tell you," Jesus answered, "before Abraham was born, _____" (John 8:58).

"_____; whoever enters through me will be saved" (John 10:9).

"_____. The good shepherd lays down his life for the sheep" (John 10:11).

"Jesus said to her, '_____. The one who believes in me will live, even though they die; and whoever lives by believing in me will never die. Do you believe this?'" (John 11:25–26).

"Jesus answered, '_____. No one comes to the Father except through me'" (John 14:6).

"_____, and my Father is the gardener" (John 15:1).

The last "I Am" statement, "I am the true vine," leads into our final section of the phases of discipleship: "Remain in Me."

Scripture of Challenge/Encouragement:

> After this the Lord appointed seventy-two others and sent them two by two ahead of him to every town and place where he was about to go. He told them, "The harvest is plentiful, but the workers are few. Ask the Lord of the harvest, therefore, to send out workers into his harvest field. Go! I am sending you out like lambs among wolves." (Luke 10:1–3)

Prayer: Meditate on the Luke passage, then write out a prayer asking God where He wants you to go to make disciples.

WEEK 14

ဢ

REMAIN IN ME

Last week we talked about going a new way. Since your last meeting, *what insights did God give you about this topic?*

This last phase of discipleship, "Remain in Me," encompassed Jesus's final few hours with His disciples before He was crucified. Between the events of the Last Supper and Jesus's capture by Roman soldiers in the garden of Gethsemane, Jesus seized the moments afforded Him for final instruction to His men. He also prepared them, as much as possible, for His impending departure.

John writes, "It was just before the Passover Festival. Jesus knew that the hour had come for him to leave this world and go to the Father. Having loved his own who were in the world, he loved them to the end" (John 13:1). Part of His final instruction to the disciples was to teach them what it meant to be a Christlike leader, to truly love others.

To teach His concept of love and leadership, Jesus, ever the consistent One, continued to use paradoxes as a style of teaching. A paradox is "a statement that is seemingly contradictory or opposed to common sense and yet is, perhaps, true" (*Merriam-Webster* online dictionary). For example, Jesus taught that one must die to live, give to receive, be enslaved to be free, walk by faith not sight, and serve to lead. Jesus embodied each of these lessons in His daily routine and life. During the final Passover meal, He taught the Twelve the lesson of leading by serving others. Read John 13:2–17 and then answer the following questions.

What exactly did Jesus do when He taught that we must serve in order to lead?

How did Peter respond to Jesus washing his feet?

In verse 10, Jesus answered Peter by saying, "A person who has had a bath needs only to wash his feet; his whole body is clean." What did He mean?

Did Jesus wash Judas Iscariot's feet, knowing he had betrayed Him? What does this teach us?

In verses 12–17, Jesus explained Himself to the disciples to further impress upon them this lesson of leading by serving. What did Jesus tell the disciples?

How can we apply Jesus's teaching to disciple-making?

After the Passover meal, Jesus began to prepare the disciples for His departure. To comfort them, Jesus said, "Do not let your hearts be troubled. You believe in God; believe also in me. My Father's house has many rooms; if that were not so, would I have told you that I am going there to prepare a place for you? And if I go and prepare a place for you, I will come back and take you to be with me that you also may be where I am. You know the way to the place where I am going" (John 14:1–4).

Then Jesus also reassured them with the promise of the coming Holy Spirit. He said, "And I will ask the Father, and he will give you another advocate to help you and be with you forever—the Spirit of truth" (John 14:16–17). As Jesus and the disciples walked to the garden of Gethsemane, He began to teach them about abiding in Him, remaining in Him. Read John 15:1–17 and then answer the following questions.

What metaphor did Jesus use to explain the relationship between the believer, the Son, and the Father? Who is who?

What is the purpose of this metaphor? In other words, what did He teach them by comparing Himself to the vine and believers to the branches?

Why was this a fitting concept the disciples would easily have understood? See the following verses for help with your answer: Psalm 80:8–19, Isaiah 4:2, 5:1–7, 53:2, and Jeremiah 33:15–16.

How many times did Jesus use the word "remain" (abide) or the phrase "remain in Me" or "abide in Me"?

According to these verses in John 15, what did Jesus mean by "remaining in Him"? (vv. 4–5, 7, 8, 10, 11, 14, 17).

Verse 2 speaks of pruning those who bear fruit. What does it mean to be pruned by the Lord? See also 1 Peter 1:6–7 and Hebrews 12:7–11.

Verse 3 says, "You are already clean." What do you think that means? See also Ephesians 5:26 and Hebrews 4:12.

John 15:4–5 says, "No branch can bear fruit by itself." What does that mean? What is the fruit this verse speaks of? See Galatians 5:22, Ephesians 5:9, and Philippians 1:10–11.

According to John 15:8, what is the result of bearing fruit? What is the result of not bearing fruit? (See John 15:2.)

What is promised in John 15:7? How does this correlate with verse 5: "Apart from me you can do nothing"? See also John 14:13.

Verses 10 and 17 support each other in establishing the correlation between obedience and love. Explain the correlation. See also James 1:22.

According to John 15:11, how is the believer completed by having knowledge of these verses? See also Romans 15:13 and Nehemiah 8:10.

According to John 15:14, what relationship status can one achieve through obedience to Christ? See Job 16:20–21 and James 4:4.

Memorizing other verses of Scripture in both the Old and New Testaments would greatly benefit us and remind us to remain in Him. Look up the following verses and record how each will help us remain in Him.

Matthew 6:33:

Psalm 27:8:

Psalm 105:4:

Psalm 63:1:

Colossians 3:1–2:

Remaining in Christ or abiding in Christ is vital to accomplishing our task of making disciples of all nations. John 15:5 is key. It says, "If a man remains in me and I in him, he will bear much fruit; apart from me you can do nothing." We must live in such a way that, apart from Him, we can do nothing.

In part 3, "The Charge: Practicing Discipleship," we have studied five phases of discipleship Jesus practiced: Come and See; Come, Follow Me; Go, Be Like Me; Go a New Way; and Remain in Me. In our examination of these phases, we have studied Jesus's earthly ministry centered on the Twelve.

Have these Scriptures been more of a challenge for you or more of an encouragement to keep doing what you are already doing to disciple others? Please explain.

Who is discipling you?

Who are you discipling?

Scripture of Challenge/Encouragement:

> How beautiful on the mountains are the feet of those who bring good news, who proclaim peace, who bring good tidings, who proclaim salvation, who say to Zion, "Your God reigns!" (Isaiah 52:7)

> The Spirit of the Sovereign LORD is on me, because the LORD has anointed me to proclaim good news to the poor. He has sent me to bind up the brokenhearted, to proclaim freedom for the captives and release from darkness for the prisoners, to proclaim the year of the LORD's favor and the day of vengeance of our God, to comfort all who mourn, and provide for those who grieve in Zion—to bestow on them a crown of beauty instead of ashes, the oil of joy instead of mourning, and a garment of praise instead of a spirit of despair. They will be called oaks of righteousness, a planting of the LORD for the display of his splendor. (Isaiah 61:1–3)

Prayer: Meditate on the passages from Isaiah, then write out a prayer thanking God for His continued provision of grace to spread the good news. Ask Him to show you where to go and who specifically to tell.

ॐ

AN OLD TESTAMENT EXAMPLE OF DISCIPLESHIP

One who has unreliable friends soon comes to ruin, but there is a friend who sticks closer than a brother. (Proverbs 18:24)

As iron sharpens iron, so one person sharpens another. (Proverbs 27:17)

WEEK 15

ॐ

ELIJAH DISCIPLES ELISHA

Last week we talked about remaining in Jesus. Since your last meeting, what insights did God give you about this topic?

Elijah's time had come to an end, and he needed to pass the baton of leadership of the Israelites to the younger prophet, Elisha. Before God took Elijah up in a whirlwind, the two of them, along with the company of prophets, journeyed from one city to three other cities before God's chariots of fire swept Elijah up to heaven. Each of these cities holds value and significance for the Israelites because they are milestones of preceding Israelite generations. Therefore, these milestones are significant to us as well as we journey together through this blessed adventure of the Christian life, being disciples and making disciples.

Let's go back to the time when Elisha was first appointed and briefly trace his journey from city to city until his final days with Elijah. Then we will see how each of these steps applies to you and me.

The Appointment

Elisha's appointment was God's plan for him. God told Elijah to "anoint Elisha, son of Shaphat from Abel Meholah to succeed you as prophet" (1 Kings 19:16). God has a plan for all of us to build His kingdom, to make disciples.

Ephesians 2:10 says, "For we are God's handiwork, created in Christ Jesus to do good works, which God prepared in advance for us to do."

Have you discerned God's purpose and plan for you to fulfill the Great Commission?

Crumb of Encouragement: Psalm 32:8. (Write it out.)

The Invitation

In a unique way, Elijah invited Elisha to minister with him: "Elijah went up to him and threw his cloak around him" (1 Kings 19:19). God also invites us to partner with Him in ministry by inviting us into the Church. Then we can help carry out kingdom work by sharing the gospel and discipling others. We can choose either to accept or reject God's invitation, which comes by His grace to us.

Hebrews 10:24–25 instructs and encourages believers to join together. It reads, "And let us consider how we may spur one another on toward love and good deeds, not giving up meeting together, as some are in the habit of doing, but encouraging one another . . ." Acts 14:27 speaks of a gathered church giving testimony of God's work through them—"them" being the local church. It says, "They gathered the church together and reported all that God had done through them and how he had opened a door of faith to the Gentiles."

How are you actively serving in the local church and allowing God to use you for His kingdom work?

Crumb of Encouragement: John 12:26. (Write it out.)

The Commitment

Elisha quickly decided to commit to the mission. Will you do likewise, or are you merely interested in connection? Commitment is never a light decision, nor does it come without cost. Elisha demonstrated the extent of his commitment when he slaughtered his oxen, burned his plow, and left his family in order to go with Elijah (1 Kings 19:21).

The believers in the early church displayed a commitment similar to Elisha as they sold their goods and gave to others as needed, according to Acts 2:45. They also "devoted themselves to the apostles' teaching and to the fellowship, to the breaking of bread and to prayer" (Acts 2:42). Their level of commitment is a challenge to twenty-first century Christianity because the world offers much to distract and entangle us from God's purpose and plan.

What is the Holy Spirit encouraging you to let go of and leave behind in order to completely commit to the purpose and plan God has called you to?

Crumb of Encouragement:

> Therefore, since we are surrounded by such a great cloud of witnesses, let us throw off everything that hinders and the sin that so easily entangles. And let us run with perseverance the race marked out for us, fixing our eyes on Jesus, the pioneer and perfecter of faith. For the joy set before him he endured the cross, scorning its shame, and sat down at the right hand of the throne of God. Consider him who endured such opposition from sinners, so that you will not grow weary and lose heart. (Hebrews 12:1–3)

Underline the instructional encouragement in these verses from Hebrews.

The Journey

Elijah and Elisha spent their last day together on the road. The places they visited held historical and spiritual significance for the Israelites. This journey represents our day-to-day living; it's a picture of discipleship (2 Kings 2:1–15).

They left Gilgal and walked first to Bethel, then to Jericho. Last, they crossed the Jordan River on dry ground. Their journey together—Elijah's final mentoring of Elisha—offers us encouragement as we journey with another, making a disciple along the way. Their relationship during their trip teaches us how to journey with others, what we should do together, what we should expect along the way, and how we should overcome obstacles together as we encourage one another to live in victory and to seek the abundant life Jesus promised.

Gilgal

"Elijah and Elisha were on their way from Gilgal" (2 Kings 2:1). Read Joshua 4:19–24, 5:9 to discover what Gilgal represents for the Israelites. Not only is the place significant, but the name Gilgal is too. It means "rolling" or "rolled away." Joshua 5:9 says, "Today I have rolled away the reproach of Egypt from you." What does "the reproach of Egypt" refer to?

In light of this verse, why was leaving Gilgal significant to Elijah and Elisha's journey?

Read 1 Peter 2:1–2. How do these verses support the representation of Gilgal?

What does "leaving Gilgal" have to do with being a disciple and making disciples?

Crumb of Encouragement: Joshua 1:9. (Write it out.)

Bethel

"So they went down to Bethel" (2 Kings 2:2). Read Genesis 28:16–22 to understand what Bethel represents for the Israelites.

According to verses 17 and 19, what significance does Bethel hold for the Israelites?

The name Bethel confirms the significance of the place itself. It means house of God, presence of God. Jacob experienced God at that place and worshiped Him there. What significance does going to Bethel hold, not only for Elijah and Elisha on their journey, but for you and me in our journeys of making disciples?

Look up Psalm 122:1. How does this verse support the significance of going to Bethel?

"Then Jacob made a vow . . . 'on this journey I am taking . . . and this stone that I have set up as a pillar will be God's house'" (Genesis 28:20, 22). That stone is symbolic of Christ because He is our Rock—the Rock of our faith.

Crumb of Encouragement: Psalm 62:2. (Write it out.)

Jericho

"So they went to Jericho" (2 Kings 2:4). Read Joshua 6:1–20 to understand Jericho's significance. Elijah and Elisha's trip to Jericho on their last day together provides several discipleship lessons for us.

What strategy did God give Joshua and the Israelites, and who was involved?

What was the result?

When we walk together, circling the promise of God, listening, and then shouting, the stronghold of the enemy will collapse before us (Joshua 6:2).

What does "going to Jericho" have to do with being a disciple and making disciples?

Read 2 Corinthians 10:3–5 and Ephesians 6:10–18. According to these verses, what weapons can we use to break down the strongholds of the enemy? And who is our enemy?

How do these verses, along with the passage from Joshua 6, encourage and help us to be a disciple and to make disciples?

Crumb of Encouragement: 2 Timothy 1:7. (Write it out.)

Crossing the Jordan River

"So the two of them walked on" (2 Kings 2:6). "Elijah and Elisha had stopped at the Jordan. Elijah took his cloak, rolled it up and struck the water with it. The water divided to the right and to the left and the two of them crossed over on dry ground" (2 Kings 2:7–8).

Read Joshua 3:9–17 (especially verses 1, 11, 15, and 17). For Elijah and Elisha, what is the significance of traveling to the Jordan and crossing it on dry ground? Crossing the Jordan River meant entering Canaan; it was fulfillment of a promise God had made to Abraham (Genesis 15:17). This land was for his descendants, and God reiterated that same promise to Moses (Exodus 3:17). So crossing the Jordan represents victory and living in victory.

What does "crossing the Jordan River" have to do with being a disciple and making disciples?

Look up John 10:10 and Romans 8:31–37. How do these verses support the promise of living in victory in Christ?

Crumb of Encouragement: Isaiah 43:1–3. (Write it out.)

As we read of Elisha and Elijah's journey, we hear three phrases repeated. At each stop (2 Kings 2, 4, and 6), Elijah told Elisha, "Stay here." Each time Elisha responded, "As surely as the LORD lives and as you live, I will not leave you." The company of prophets also asked Elisha, "Do you know that the LORD is going to take your master from you today?" (2 Kings 2:3, 5). What do you think was the purpose of these verbal exchanges at each place?

Elijah told Elisha, "Stay here." I think he wanted to test Elisha, to challenge him to examine himself and his commitment—to count the cost. It's similar to what Naomi first told Ruth: "Go back" and "Return home" (Ruth 1:8, 11, 12).

This is the same thing Christ said to the crowds following Him and to us: count the cost (Luke 14:25–35). Each time Elisha responded ("As surely as the LORD lives and as you live, I will never leave you"), he confirmed his commitment. He had made his decision, and he was prepared to follow. Ruth responded to Naomi the same way: "Where you go, I will go" (Ruth 1:16). Disciples of Christ should do likewise; this is Jesus's expectation of us. Where He goes, we go (we follow). And He expects us to lead others to do the same.

The company of prophets, which was probably more like a ministry school, kept asking Elisha if he knew the Lord was going to take his master today. Why? Perhaps to keep Elisha focused. He needed to prepare himself for Elijah's departure and the new leadership role he himself would soon undertake. He had to be ready, to be prepared. In much the same way, Paul instructed Timothy in 2 Timothy 4:2, "Be prepared in season and out of season." Paul's instructions to Timothy are meant for us too. We are to be prepared with the gospel at all times. Peter gave similar instructions: "But in your hearts revere Christ as Lord. Always be prepared to give an answer to everyone who asks you to give the reason for the hope that you have" (1 Peter 3:15).

In their conversation at the Jordan River, Elijah asked Elisha, "Tell me, what can I do for you before I am taken from you?" (2 Kings 2:9). Elisha responded, "Let me inherit a double portion of your spirit" (2 Kings 2:9). What does that mean? What was Elisha asking of Elijah? A double portion was the birthright of the firstborn in Hebrew culture. Elisha asked for Elijah's anointing to be duplicated in his, for Elijah's ministry to be manifested doubly in Elisha's ministry. Interestingly but not surprisingly, the Bible records that Elisha did twice as many miracles as Elijah: Elisha's twenty-eight, compared to Elijah's fourteen.

Elijah and Elisha's mentor-mentee relationship serves as a model for you and me as we learn and practice the discipling of others. It is a reminder to leave behind a legacy of faith for each generation to lead the next. "One generation commends your works to another; they will tell of your mighty acts" (Psalm 145:4). From those more mature in the Lord, we learn to leave sin behind, worship the Lord, use the weapons of God to break down strongholds of the enemy, and by God's grace walk with one another, living victorious in Christ Jesus. It's our responsibility to pass on this faith through discipleship.

Scripture of Challenge/Encouragement:

> We will not hide them from their descendants; we will
> tell the next generation the praiseworthy deeds of the
> LORD, his power, and the wonders he has done. (Psalm
> 78:4)

Prayer: Meditate on the verse from Psalms, then write out a prayer of thanks to God for the person or persons who led you to Christ and for those who are discipling you. And ask God to help you boldly tell and lead the next generation to follow and proclaim the wonders of our God and Savior, Jesus Christ.

PART 5 (INDIVIDUAL STUDY)

ℰℭ

A Testimony of Discipleship

Denver Moore's definition of friendship from Same Kind of Different as Me:

Being friends is like being soldiers in the army. You live together; you fight together; you die together. I knowed Mr. Ron wadn't fixin to come up outta no bushes and help me fight. But then I got to thinkin about him some more and thought maybe we might have somethin to offer each other. I could be his friend in a different way than he could be my friend. I knowed he wanted to help the homeless, and I could take him places he couldn't go by hisself. I didn't know what I might find in his circle or even that I had any business bein there, but I knowed he could help me find out whatever was down that road.

The way I looked at it, a fair exchange ain't no robbery, and a even swap ain't no swindle. He was gon' protect me in country club, and I was gon' protect him in the hood. Even swap, straight down the line.

If you is lookin for a real friend, then I'll be one. Forever.[34]

WEEK 16

༚

FRIENDSHIP TO DISCIPLESHIP, BY CHRISTY MOONEY

My definition of discipleship is one person initially learning from the other, and then two people learning from each other. In my experience, it started out just like that. Here is my story.

I was living a good life: a good marriage, two healthy kids, a nice home, and a decent job. I felt happy. I was enjoying my life, or so I thought. About this time I was invited to go to an out-of-state women's conference. One night after the worship service, one of my dear friends shared some personal struggles with me and asked for my advice. I didn't know how to help her, but I said, "Let me run and get someone who can help."

I raced to Ellie's room and got her out of bed. Later, as I sat back and listened to the two of them talk, I heard the Lord speak to my heart. He told me I was lukewarm. I knew from Scripture that this was not a good place to be: "So, because you are lukewarm—neither hot nor cold—I am about to spit you out of my mouth" (Revelation

3:16). I was basically a fence-sitter with one foot in the world, one foot in the Word. I made a decision that day that I would no longer be a lukewarm, fence-sitting Christian.

So my journey began. I began learning all I possibly could learn from Ellie, asking lots of questions, watching how she waited on the Lord's answers, and basically observing how she lived out life. What I was doing is biblical. Hebrews 13:7 says, "Remember your leaders who spoke the word of God to you. Consider the outcome of their way of life and imitate their faith." You see, at this point I was weak in my faith, but I soon learned that when I am weak, God's power is strong. "But he said to me, 'My grace is sufficient for you, for my power is made perfect in weakness'" (2 Corinthians 12:9). I have learned not to be so upset by my weakness if I am seeking God's will. That's when He can use me the most.

Before this time in my life, I was unaware of God's grace, mercy, power, and love. With much observation and studying, I discovered all those attributes of my loving Father. Ellie gave me a bag full of books, and I started reading *Lord, I Need Grace to Make It Today,* by Kay Arthur. Each of those books had personal notes written through them. It meant a lot that she would share such personal information with me. I went from finishing those books to reading the New Testament in *The Message* version of the Bible and making notes. Then I bought many more books on my own that would teach me more about my Lord. My Savior soon became my best friend.

In our journey of friendship, Ellie has discipled me in key areas of the Christian life. We went on a beach trip together early in our friendship. That was one of the first times I watched her to see how she did things. She was the first one up and out the door to find a quiet place to meet with the Lord. She has taught me how she studies. She usually reads a Psalm prior to anything else she's planning to study. This has led me to do the same.

She has taught me how to pray simply by praying with me. She never starts a prayer without first telling God who He is to her. This changes each time she prays. She truly reflects the model prayer in Matthew. This has taught me to do the same. God is something different to each of us, and we must tell Him who He is to us. We also pray together for each other and our families.

Ellie has taught me about fellowship in a meaningful way. When we talk, she always asks how my family is, how my day is going, just to let me know she cares. That approach has spilled over in my life and my fellowship with others, because people don't care what you know until they know that you care. Ellie taught me to be intentional because fellowship is so important.

I've watched her witness simply by living life: loving people, not appearing judgmental, and having a boldness to share God's Word. She has spoken at our church's women's conference for the past four years, and each time I've watched her fight through nerves to share God's Word. Everyone who has ever heard her speak loves her! People often say her passion exhausts her. When you are tired from worshiping, that's good stuff. That's how she witnesses to me.

As I started attending women's conferences and Christian concerts with other Christ-followers, God began weeding out some of my daily activities, like certain TV shows, and then He changed my taste in music. Ellie encouraged me to listen to "Jesus music," saying, "If you don't know the words to the songs, listen until you do, and then you will like it." I did, and guess what? Now that's all I listen to. I have been so blessed by this because what I listen to, my kids listen to—and learn. I have also grown to love God's Word. My favorite verse is Psalm 37:4: "Take delight in the LORD, and he will give you the desires of your heart."

As I put pins in my Jesus road-trip map, growing in my faith and allowing God to shape me and mold me into who He wants me to be,

Ellie encouraged me to step out of my comfort zone and teach our young adult Bible fellowship class. Initially I hesitated, but she assured me I could do it. She told me she knew I would pray and seek the Lord, and the lesson would come from Him.

Disciple-makers don't have to be perfect. Ellie is not perfect; she's real. She has flaws and imperfections, and she messes up like everyone else. However, God's Word and His will are perfect and without flaw (Romans 12:2). I have watched her and know that she reads and studies the Word daily. What an example for me. Now I am that example to my own kids because they watch me. As much as I love her as my best friend, I am reminded how much more my Father in heaven loves me.

In this journey, I have and I am discipling others. I have developed some close relationships with a few women I can pour into, encourage, pray for, and discuss Scripture with. I also teach Girls in Action, a mission group for elementary girls, but it's more than just lessons. I have developed relationships with these little girls and their moms through get-togethers and service projects. I have grown. I have also failed at times, but God restores me each time I come to Him. I am so thankful for everyone who helped disciple me. Be a disciple, live like a disciple, and be a disciple-maker.

It takes one to make one.

It's an investment, not a project.

Always set them up to win!

Thanks be to Jesus!

I always thank my God as I remember you
in my prayers, because I hear about your love
for all his holy people and your faith in the Lord Jesus.
I pray that your partnership with us in the faith
may be effective in deepening your understanding
of every good thing we share for the sake of Christ.
Your love has given me great joy and encouragement,
because you, brother, have refreshed the hearts of the Lord's people.
(Philemon 1:4–7)

May these words of my mouth and this
meditation of my heart
be pleasing in your sight,
LORD, my Rock and my
Redeemer.
(Psalm 19:14)

ENDNOTES

[1] Vernon McGee, *Thru the Bible with J. Vernon McGee: Volume IV Matthew–Romans* (Tennessee: Thomas Nelson, 1983), 467.

[2] Bill Hull, *Jesus Christ, Disciplemaker* (Michigan: Baker Books, 2007), 188.

[3] Dietrich Bonhoeffer, *The Cost of Discipleship* (New York: Touchstone, 1995), 88–89.

[4] Hull, *Jesus Christ*, 220.

[5] David Platt, *Radical: Taking Back Your Faith from the American Dream* (New York: Multnomah, 2011), 11–12.

[6] Bonhoeffer, *The Cost*, 44–45.

[7] Bonhoeffer, *The Cost*, 50–51.

[8] Bonhoeffer, *The Cost*, 45.

[9] Hull, *Jesus Christ*, 140.

[10] Adelle M. Banks, "The Bible–Helpful, but Not Read Much," LifeWay Research, April 25, 2017, https://cruxnow.com/.../04/27/americans-bible-helpful-not-read-much. Accessed June 2017.

[11] Hull, *Jesus Christ*, 92.

[12] A. W. Tozer, *The Radical Cross: Living the Passion of Christ* (Pennsylvania: Wing-spread, 2006). Accessed online August 2018.

[13] Hull, *Jesus Christ*, 94.

[14] Hull, *Jesus Christ*, 108.

[15] Platt, *Radical*, 156.

[16] Platt, *Radical*, 157.

[17] Bonhoeffer, *The Cost*, 84.

[18] Bonhoeffer, *The Cost*, 63–64.

[19] Platt, *Radical*, 72–73.

[20] Bible Lexicon - Bible Hub, https://biblehub.com/lexicon/.

[21] Hull, *Jesus Christ*, 121–122.

[22] Hull, *Jesus Christ*, 115.

[23] Hull, *Jesus Christ*, 169.

[24] Tom Minor (former pastor of South Shelby Baptist Church), interviewed by Ellie Littleton, Shelby, Alabama, December 31, 2013, transcript, "Book of Minorisms."

[25] Hull, *Jesus Christ*, 33.

[26] Hull, *Jesus Christ*, 31–32.

27 Hull, *Jesus Christ*, 33–34.
28 Hull, *Jesus Christ*, 41.
29 Hull, *Jesus Christ*, 80.
30 Hull, *Jesus Christ*, 81–82.
31 Hull, *Jesus Christ*, 83.
32 Platt, *Radical*, 100–101.
33 Hull, *Jesus Christ*, 103.
34 Ron Hall and Denver Moore, *Same Kind of Different as Me* (Tennessee: Thomas Nelson, 2006), 108–109.

Ellie's first Bible study group at her home studying
Be a Disciple, Make a Disciple.

Order Information

To order additional copies of this book, please visit
www.redemption-press.com.
Also available on Amazon.com and
BarnesandNoble.com
Or by calling toll free 1-844-2REDEEM.